Buck Hill
A History

Let's Give It A Whirl!

⋀⋀⋀

Nancy Campbell Stone

This is a work of nonfiction. The events and conversations in this book have been set down to the best of the author's ability, although some names and details may have been changed to protect the privacy of individuals. Any resemblance to persons living or dead should be plainly apparent to them and those who know them, especially if the author has provided their real names.

Buck Hill A History
Let's Give it a Whirl!

By Nancy Campbell Stone

First paperback edition 2019.
Printed in the United States of America.

ISBN 978-0-578-59278-7

Library of Congress Control Number:2019916245

Author Contact:
jessicastone@me.com

Printed at:
Smith Printing Co. LLC
17343 Wolverine St. NW
Ramsey, MN 55303
Phone: 763-241-9613
Toll Free (USA): 1-800-416-9099

Table of Contents

** Denotes that this person has written a personal memory to be found
in the Memories section of this book.*

FOREWORD

To the reader: Here I am in the Baker Library at Dartmouth College on August 2, 1999. I might be sitting in the same chair once occupied by Chuck Stone in the early fifties. I am embarking on an unfamiliar project of writing a history of a small ski area in Minnesota.

Sixteen years later, in 2015, after we sold Buck Hill, I became serious about writing this history of the ups and downs of the ski business. To the best of my recollection this is how it all happened from September of 1954 to October of 2015. Let me say in advance, there are many employees and guests that were very important to us at Buck Hill which I may have unintentionally left out. Please forgive me and thank you all for your contributions to this unique enterprise known as Buck Hill. Buck Hill, Inc. also included Powder Ridge and there is some Powder Ridge history mentioned in this book as well.

ᴧᴧᴧ

The Bucket Chalet, built mostly by Glen Stanley.

ACKNOWLEDGMENTS

The task of writing this Buck Hill History would have been much different if Chuck Stone had not saved all newspaper articles, plans, board minutes, financial reports, drawings, letters and pictures pertaining to Buck Hill. I didn't have to search very far for information.

This book would have been impossible for me to write without the expertise and ongoing editing, typing, dependable support and input of Colleen Crawford. Others made important contributions including Tom Traub who read the script many times, and had insightful suggestions with grammar and how to make the book more readable, and Janet Holmgren who also helped with the editing, and, was, an, expert, at, removing, commas.

Members of my family who were especially helpful include my daughters, Jessica (Wiltgen) Stone and Polly Hanson, who wrote the Buck Hill Ski Team history. My granddaughter, Madeline Wiltgen, helped extensively by sorting and organizing 61 years of papers and documents. My grandson, Charlie Hanson, helped with some editing and had important critiques. Most of the photographs are from our family collection and were taken by Chuck Stone, Charles Stone, III and Jessica Stone. My granddaughter Emily Stone[*], did some drawings as well. My cousin Jonathan Horton, who's creativity and craftsmanship was integral to Frightmares, remembered details from those exciting years. My brother Stuart Campbell shared precious memories of the early years, the employees, and some very funny stories including the struggles and successes we all had together.

Ski area managers Don McClure and Jerry Wahlin each provided valuable information about the mechanics of operating the ski areas. Other employees who were very helpful were (in alphabetical order) Steve Bauer, Leslie Callahan, Tom Hayden, Ron Heneman, Tom Schulz and Julie Welsh. Kerstin Hammarberg who has been the Buck Hill Ski Patrol Director since 2005 has provided us with many of the ski patrol pictures.

Erich and Ursula Sailer, their daughter Martina Sailer Cook, and Tasha Nelson McCrank were very helpful in providing information on the USSA ski team. I am sorry that we could not mention every racer because they were all so important to the program and I believe are expert skiers forever.

I also want to thank Caroline MacWherter, Holly Traub and David (Rip) West who each made a unique contribution for making this book possible.

Carly Kirk at Cornerstone Copy Center has been incredibly helpful at putting all of the words and pictures together. And believe me, that's not an easy task!

I tried my best to track down every employee that I remembered from the past as I knew their memories would be invaluable to this story. I know there are many of you that I missed and I want you to know we are very grateful for your contributions to the success of Buck Hill.

This book is dedicated to the memory of Chuck Stone.

The Last Ice Age to the 1950's

Remains of a Glacier, Early History, Gokey Hill, Fred Pabst, Marjorie Benedikter, A Christmas Gift, Lake Harriett Park

Blizz, Buck, and Whirly looking for a ski hill.

Ten Thousand Years ago the last ice age receded from the northern half of the North American continent. The Minnesota River helped drain that glacier and a terminal moraine formed south of the river. Today the remnant of the glacier is called Buck Hill. It is the highest point in an approximately 200-mile radius surrounding Buck Hill at 1,210 feet above sea level, with a 313 foot vertical rise. Near the base of the hill large bands of Chippewa Native Americans pitched their teepees on the shores of Crystal Lake, or "Minne Elk" as they called it. The Native Americans named the hill, Buck's Hill. From the top of the hill they could look down at their village and surrounding areas. This is where they hunted and watched for deer as they came to drink at the lake. The well traveled game trail that led from the Minnesota River to points further south is now, a mere century and a half later, a major freeway-35W with 80,000 cars passing by each day. Above the freeway to the west, is a special hill where every year well over l70,000 skiers and snowboarders pursue their favorite winter sports.

Buck Hill was first opened briefly, in the 1930's, by Gokeys Sporting Goods store in St. Paul and was known as Gokey Hill at that time. Gokeys was one of the only stores to sell alpine ski equipment and thus needed a place for their customers to use their new skis. There was little snow during the dust bowl years of the 1930's and the skiers had to walk half a mile from old Lyndale Avenue to Gokey Hill. In 1937, the Buck Hill land was assigned to Grace A. Whittier, the daughter of a Northfield banker, who had bought the land for payment of back taxes in the mid 30's. In 1939, an easement on the property was assigned to Northern Natural Gas. Grace continued to own the land until her death in 1984.

Northland Ski Manufacturing Co. got it's start in St. Paul in 1912

On February 11, 1938 an article in *The Ski Bulletin* on Central Skiing stated that "On February 6th, an installation of a ski tow had been completed at Minneapolis' new ski development at Buck Hill, near Orchard Gardens, MN, but lack of snow had made it a poor season. Skiing had not been a big success in Minnesota that winter. The fields had been swept clear of snow, and what drifts were left were as grey as the fields until one night, when it rained, then snowed, so the trees were an inch deep with white in the morning."

The next attempt to open the area for skiing was undertaken by Fred Pabst of the Pabst Brewing family who leased the land from Grace Whittier. Mr. Pabst had planned a chain of ski areas across the country. Though he started several, by

2015 only three remained open for business with new owners: Big Bromley in Vermont, Rib Mountain (Granite Peak) in Wisconsin and Buck Hill. On December 7, 1941 as a crew was stringing a rope on the hill, they heard that Pearl Harbor had been attacked and work immediately stopped. It would be another thirteen years before Chuck Stone started the modern Buck Hill.

Marjorie Benedikter, who operated Moon Valley Ski Area near Shakopee, intended to lease and reopen Buck Hill in 1949. Her plans changed when she was offered the head designer position for White Stag Ski Apparel in Seattle, Washington. Even though Marjorie never opened the area, she did make an essential contribution to the future of Buck Hill. She talked the highway department into rerouting Highway 65 (Interstate 35W) around the hill, rather than through it, which would have destroyed the property and the hill. We were grateful to Marjorie for this major contribution.

Marjorie Benedikter on the Moon Valley brochure in 1949.

My love of skiing started when we were living in south Minneapolis, across the street from Lake Harriett Park. My brother Stuart and I had each received a pair of skis for Christmas in 1947. In March of 1948, my sophomore year, the teachers went on strike at Southwest High School. This was a year of plentiful snow and with school not in session it was just right for learning to ski. The Hancock brothers and I would scurry over to the park every day, build jumps on the tiny hill (at the time we thought it was huge) and ski straight down. We had long wooden skis, with a very primitive binding, that usually held the toe in place. They were Lund's or Northland skis. The strike ended too soon and I was hooked on skiing. Little did I know then that skiing would become a major influence in my life and since then I have been privileged to ski at over 150 ski areas.

THE FIFTIES

*Sun Valley, A New Sport, Finding Buck Hill,
Grace Whittier, Skiing Boom, Friends and Exploits,
Ski Racing, A Proposal, Early Years, A Stock Sale*

Possibly the first snowfall in 1954 with the original trail map.

In 1952 during my junior year at the University of Minnesota, I heard there were jobs available at Sun Valley for the winter season, so I took the streetcar over to the Union Pacific offices in St. Paul and applied for a job. I assured my parents

that I could make up the time in summer school, which I did. I got a job at the Round House, which was the warming chalet and restaurant mid-way up the Mountain. It was the ideal place to work. Sun Valley paid our train fare from Minnesota and back plus room and board and $40 every two weeks. They also paid to have our ski pants dry cleaned. The best part of the arrangement for me though, was free skiing.

My Sun Valley racing bib.

Some of the other Round House workers and I would ride the single chair lift on River Run with the Ski Patrol at 8:00 a.m. every morning to the top of Baldy (Bald) Mountain. The patrollers even yodeled to get the day started. We did not have to report for work until 11:00 a.m., which gave us a lot of time that we sorely needed to perfect our skiing. We had a rather unique way of skiing down the mountain as we had not yet learned the necessary technique of turning. My new friend, Parmela McCabe, and I would ski straight down, try to

turn and then fall again and again and again. However, I was very fortunate that most of my fellow workers at the Round House were on the U.S. Ski Team and gave me a lot of expert instruction on the Round House slope after work. By the end of the winter I could ski the whole mountain nonstop and I even did a little ski racing.

I was 20 years old and so were most of my friends and we were all blessed with a sense of humor. The boys from the far west came out to ski on weekends and holidays and they often wanted to ski with the employees after work or even take us out for dinner. It was a treat after eating at the Rec Hall every day, even though the food there was very good. One of

Skiing with Busby Vaughan and Parmela McCabe in the Sawtooth Mountains; Sun Valley 1953

our favorite tricks was to have the boys follow us down the Round House slope and then we would cut over to Olympic which had a very sharp right angle turn. We would ski to the right and stop and laugh as they kept going straight and flew into the abyss. We neglected to tell them about the turn. Fortunately, no one ever got hurt and we all had a lot of laughs. Sun Valley was a magical interlude before I headed back to the U for spring quarter of my junior year, and to meet Chuck Stone!

Chuck's introduction to skiing was the result of a serious bout with polio in the summer of 1947. He could not go back to Breck school the next fall as he was still recovering from the disease and was spending a great deal of time in physical therapy at the Sister Kenny Institute. One sunny winter day, his father decided to take him along on a short business trip that would bring them near the town of Bayport, Minnesota and a ski area called Barker's Alps. His father, in his immutable style, dropped Chuck off with instructions to learn to ski and he would be picked up at 5:00 p.m. Chuck did learn to ski that day and totally enjoyed it as his father probably knew he would.

Chuck excelled in many sports including several that he continued to enjoy for the rest of his life. When he returned to Breck School, fully recovered from his bout with polio, he was a co-captain of the football team and played on the hockey, tennis, and golf teams. After he enrolled at Dartmouth College in the fall of 1949 he found part time work at the Suicide Six Ski Area which was owned by Bunny Bertram. Upon graduation in 1953, he returned to Minneapolis and worked for his family's business as a machine tool salesman and skied and raced whenever he could. He even tried jumping at Theodore Wirth Park!

Chuck taking a break from studying at Dartmouth.

Chuck and I eventually met on a blind date at the suggestion of a mutual friend, Bill Cargill, (otherwise known as Tojo). He knew that we both loved to ski and thought we would have a lot in common to talk about. I was a junior at the University of Minnesota and living at the Kappa house and had just returned from my Sun Valley adventure. Chuck was a senior and had just returned from Aspen where he was writing his senior thesis on the history of Aspen. He was on his way back to Dartmouth and graduation where President Dwight D. Eisenhower gave his famous "book burning" speech to the class of 1953.

Our first date was at Sheik's restaurant in Minneapolis. Naturally a large part of the date was spent talking about our mutual love of skiing and racing. When I returned to the Kappa house, I was asked how the date went, as many of them knew Chuck. I responded that I was impressed that he could smoke, drink and talk all at the same time! It was a fun first date but he had to go back to Dartmouth to graduate. I spent that next summer working in Glacier National Park as a vegetable girl in the kitchen and doing a lot of hiking. The following fall, we were both asked to be in Bill Cargill's wedding party and Chuck asked me out again. Soon after, we began to date regularly. Some of those dates included local ski racing. The winter seasons of 1953-1954 and 1954-1955 Chuck and I ski raced at Halloway Hill in Detroit Lakes, Grand Marais ski area in Grand Marais, Bush Lake in Bloomington, Lone Lake in Hopkins, Lutsen, and Buck Hill of course.

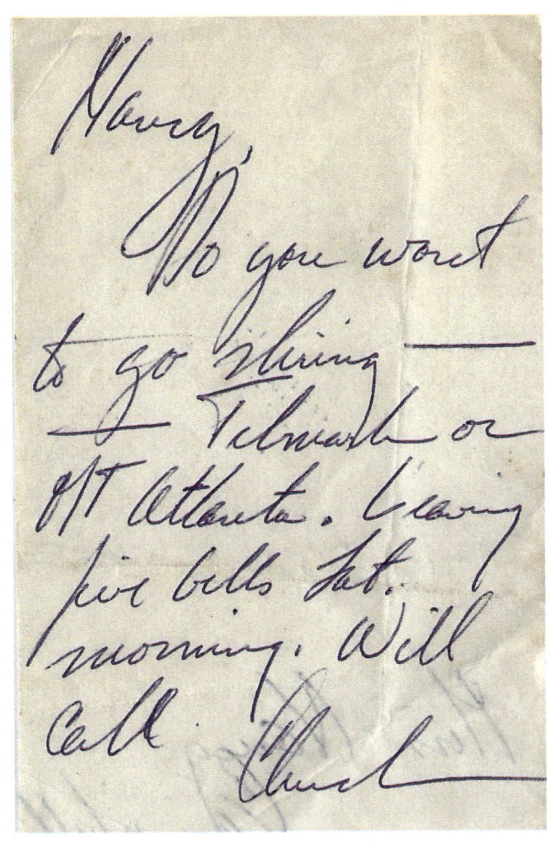

Date invite from Chuck, 1954

One day in the summer of l954, Chuck and I were having lunch in Donaldson's Tea Room, on 7th and Nicollet in downtown Minneapolis. We were reminiscing about our recent trip out west when Chuck said, "Wouldn't it be fun to own a ski area?" I was ecstatic about the whole idea. He then headed for the library to find the highest hill in the surrounding vicinity. He did just that and it turned out to be Buck Hill. After considerable investigation he discovered that Grace Whittier who lived in Northfield, Minnesota was the owner of Buck Hill. Chuck made arrangements to have a meeting with her and two evenings later we were sitting in her living room. Miss Whittier gave us a brief history of the hill, which she dearly loved. She would often spend hours hiking around the property. She told us there were other local skiing enthusiasts, who had skied the area for years, including two past Minnesota governors, but there wasn't a ski lift and they had to walk to the hill from old Lyndale Avenue. I can only speculate that it must have been our youthful enthusiasm that overwhelmed Grace as she signed a lease with us two weeks later on September 1, l954. We were in the ski business! Chuck was 23 years old and I was 22.

Grace A Whittier was a very charming and intelligent woman. She had all the qualifications of a good businesswoman and was always very fair and considerate in the many years of our relationship with her. We had negotiated a five - year lease with Grace with an option to buy the land. Our arrangement was that she receive 13% of the ticket sales each year and we would pay the taxes. I was the bookkeeper in those years and that, combined with attending to our very small children, did become overwhelming at times. Grace stayed in close touch with us and seemed to completely understand our situation, as she mentioned in a letter that she wrote to me in April, 1959. However, I must admit that, due to the lack of snowfall until the winter of l961-62, there really wasn't that much to do in the financial department. Later in 1962, Grace donated five acres of her property for a new church across the road which was named Grace Methodist Church in her honor.

Grace Methodist Church - the land donated by Grace Whittier.

Skiing was not only in its earliest stages in Minnesota, but throughout the United States as well. Organized skiing in the eastern United States began in the winter of 1933-1934 just a few miles down the road from Dartmouth College. A rope tow was run up a hillside pasture behind Gilbert's Farm on Route 12 outside the town of Woodstock, Vermont. It was the first rope tow to operate in the United States and it was always breaking down. The owner, Bunny Bertram, improved it by observing a Ferris wheel and adapting that system to the tow. Surprisingly it worked. Hill number six became Suicide Six and Bunny took in his first dollar on Christmas Day 1937. It cost $1.00 to ski all day and 50 cents for the afternoon. A season pass cost $8.00. Sir Arnold Lunn (the father of slalom) called Suicide Six the best natural slalom hill he had ever seen. Perhaps Chuck formed his idea of owning a ski area from working with Bunny Bertram.

There is little doubt that Chuck's years at Dartmouth and working at Suicide Six had a significant impact on his style of management and commitment to the traditions in skiing and ski racing. He was familiar with most of the personalities in skiing, past and present, and often spoke of the

Chuck taking some practice runs at Lutsen.

tremendous influence Dartmouth had on the growth of the industry. There were four Dartmouth men on the 1952 U.S. Olympic team that competed in Oslo Norway: Bill Beck, Brooks Dodge, Chick Igaya and David Lawrence. That was very impressive for any school. The first modern collegiate downhill race in the US was held on Mt. Moosilauke in 1933 on a 4.5 mile course with a 2,800 foot vertical drop. During his years at Dartmouth, Chuck and his friends went on many skiing weekends, sometimes as far away as Mont-Tremblant in Canada. Other areas they skied were Oak Hill in Hanover, Mad River Glen, Stowe, Franconia Notch and many others. In between these skiing weekends I think Chuck might have done some studying.

In 1954 when we went into the ski business and obtained a lease on Buck Hill, the area was completely surrounded by farmland. The road in front of the hill was two lane Highway 65. The hill itself was almost completely covered with oak and cherry trees. There were a few very narrow trails that had been cut and rudely maintained by local skiing enthusiasts over the years. There was a lot to do if we were going to open the area in December! We garnered $3,700, a lot of friends, some old cutting tools and equipment and went to work.

Looking Southeast from the top in the late 1950's.

September 1954, lots to do before the snow flies!

Clearing the trails was quite a challenge as we were using borrowed chain saws and old brush cutters. It didn't help that our weekend crew did not have any experience with those tools! Of course it all needed to be done by hand, as there were not any bulldozers or earthmoving equipment at our disposal. My brother, Stuart Campbell, and Charles and Bill McCarthy* were among the weekend clearing crew. Henry Jackson was a local farmer who was especially helpful to us, loaning us tools and lots of good advice.

Our favorite downhill course, Nancy's Folly.

Our two partners the first years were Sumner Young and Glen Stanley. Sumner was a good friend of Chuck's and Glen was his skiing coach at Breck School. Fortunately for us, Glen was a carpenter and a member of the renowned Tenth Mountain Division of World War II fame, many of which were instrumental in the rapid development of the Ski Industry after World War II. From the very beginning, Walter Bush*, Chuck's long time friend from Breck School and Dartmouth College, was our attorney and advisor in all legal matters.

We held the first board meeting on Dec. 6, 1954. The officers were: President – Chuck Stone, Vice Presidents – Glen R. Stanley, Sumner Young, Secretary/Treasurer – Nancy Campbell (we had not married yet).

We built a small chalet with Glen's professional guidance and carpentry skills which we named The Bucket. The 1,020 square ft. building contained a lunch counter, repair shop, and small sales area. It did not have the convenience of running water. Therefore, as in days gone bye, the outhouse was conveniently located back in the woods.

Nancy taking a bubble break.

Nancy Campbell, Chuck Stone, and Glen Stanley looking for snow; December 1954

A very good day in the 1960's

I recall helping with insulation and also doing a lot of painting. We made a collage on the north wall from various old ski poster collections. The early food service workers and hamburger cooks included Joan McCaull Strand, Nancy Wiegand Hirshfield, Jody Moore CoMartin, Diane Robinson, and Donna Thompson Klass. They met every challenge with determination and a smile. Because of lack of adequate refrigeration space we would sometimes put the uncooked hamburger in the snow to keep it cold. Another good friend, Sheila Murphy Nichols sold tickets and did whatever else needed to be done that first winter. We paid $1.50 an hour and all the skiing you could possibly want when and if it snowed. Our first address was Buck Hill, Orchard Gardens, Savage, Minnesota.

During that time, I clearly recall a friend who decided to sing "I'll dance at your wedding" over the loud speaker. This was before Chuck and I were engaged, so you can only imagine how embarrassed I was!

The following is a personal remembrance written by Bill McCarthy:

Summer '54 –framing the chalet. Saturday morning meant numerous trips into Lakeville to the hardware store for tools and miscellaneous items. We groomed "the run" of rocks and stones and I helped Chuck to keep that old green tractor running. It was really nuts. But it was really fun and exciting too! You and Chuck were recent college grads; I was headed back to the "U" for my senior year. Seems as though Glen Stanley was the old man in the crowd and had some ideas of how to put up a chalet. Somewhere we had gotten an old toboggan for the "ski patrol" and a way to get someone down the hill if necessary. I was the patrol and I shudder to think about it – we did have liability insurance didn't we?

Charles McCarthy liked to tell the story of Chuck going down the road to buy some dynamite to deal with a very large and persistent oak tree stump. The end result was this huge stump blown 60 feet into the air, dangling roots like tentacles on an octopus. Charles McCarthy remembers this event very well:

Albert B. Nobel patented dynamite in 1867. His creation was mixing nitroglycerin into clay, thus making nitroglycerin a practical explosive. Nitroglycerin alone is unstable and can easily explode by bumping it. Dynamite is commonly put in 8 x 1 ½ waxed cardboard tubes with crimped ends. It is so stable it requires a blasting cap lit by a fuse or electrical current to set it off (think powerful firecracker). I came to the hill one Saturday morning circa 1956 or 1957 to find Chuck in the process of "blowing a stump" which was east of the present day Daktronics digital display board and a bit north. The subject stump was an Oak over 30 inches in diameter (persons involved remember these things). In the days of real firecrackers, many of us, Chuck and I included, knew how to blow stuff up. He had hollowed a space under the stump, placed dynamite with blasting cap, packed sand back into the cavity to direct the force upward, and applied electrical current. The cap exploded – the dynamite didn't.

Chuck returned with a tidy wooden case of dynamite. I took 6 sticks, placed a cap to one, placed it under the stump, packed all the old dynamite, sand and new sand into the cavity. I stepped to my car, touched the leads to the battery and KERWHUMP, the stump rose, intact, with 8 & 10 foot roots protruding all around, rising 60-80-100 feet into the sky. It turned over, fell and bounced once and we all shut our gaping mouths. It could have ended badly, but I am proud to say that there is no stump there today. I checked. I think six sticks was enough. Those were good days. My sister Sheila was also a weekend worker in the early days.

Another fun memory of those days came from Jim Kaufman, often a member of the weekend work crew:

When Chuck Stone let out the word about starting a ski area south of Minneapolis, there was a lot of excitement. His friends (and there were many) asked what they might do to help.

Aside from a few investors, Chuck quickly found a small army of volunteers to start clearing the slopes and surrounding terrain. It became a weekend event throughout the fall, and all had a good time doing so.

Having been one of the weekend workers, I thought it would be nice to have some refreshments for the team on the ground. During an after work session, someone asked why not bring something to the workers? The idea of a parachute tethered to two six packs, delivered by plane would add some excitement. I picked up on the idea and put together a chute with bed sheet material and rope.

Jim's gift to the weekend workers. Drawing by Emily Stone.

The weather was nice the afternoon of October 30th, 1954 and I had signed up the rental of an airplane, Aeronca 7AC, number "N 3917E" with a continental 65 hp engine. My old log book still shows the entry.

From the St. Paul airport, I took off with the parachute on the passenger seat, headed SW around World Chamberlain Field (MSP Intl) with Buck Hill dead ahead. Below were the workers. With a somewhat sharp bank over the slopes, a partially opened door, (I) pushed out the chute. It opened and floated down. I could see workers running to recover the package and wildly waving to me.

As flight rules and airspace restrictions have developed, this was way out of bounds of smart behavior.

This small event was only one of the many gestures by the large group of friends who so much wanted to see the opening of Buck Hill Ski Area.

Nancy (Wiegand) Hirshfield reminded me of the time we were stacking up brush in a huge pile at the bottom of the hill. Chuck came down from the top of the hill on a small green tractor he was riding and we told him we were going to burn the brush. "No, no, no," he said, "Miss Whittier would be very upset if we burned down the hill." Off he went to the top and guess what – we burned the brush! Lucky for us there were no dire consequences and we had a roaring fire on a chilly day.

Some of us had done a little ski racing, so clearing a downhill course was a high priority. The top of the race course was squeezed in among the oak trees

and the run was called Nancy's Folly. It was another tight fit at the bottom to find the finish line. A lot of the time those races were held on very marginal snow. Today's racers would be astounded!

I also remember one night in early December when Chuck and I were working in the chalet. The area had been open that day and there had been a race on Nancy's Folly. Our Vampire skis were standing in the

A view from Nancy's Folly. Notice Hwy 65.

snow outside. We heard a car engine and went out to check and the skis were gone. We called it quits for the night and amazingly when we went out the door our skis had been returned, perhaps by our guardian snow angel. Skis were a major purchase in those days and they still are today.

Ski Racing became an institution very early in Buck Hill's history. The enthusiasm of local racers never faltered even when during the season of 1953-1954, not one event was held due to lack of snow. On December 14, 1954 the Buck Hill Slalom Club was formed with the purpose of promoting downhill and slalom racing. President of the club was Fred Lang: Vice President - Bob Tengdin, Treasurer- Ken Dean, and Secretary - Pat Gleason. The entire program of the Buck Hill Club consisted of preparing for and entering races and encouraging non-racers to do the same. Meetings were informal sessions held on the slopes with old hands like Bill "Beetle" Campbell, Midge Dean, Ken Hancock, Hans Hopf, Fred Lang, Irv Kilstoffe, Bill Lamb, Bob Tengdin, Tom Vitala, Pat Gleason and others. Future plans of the club included bringing more young racers into the racing circuit and a slalom clinic at Buck Hill. This would include a special demonstration by "Kansas" Tengdin on the art

Glen, Nancy, and Chuck getting ready to take some runs.

Bob Sanderson is presented with the Bucket trophy.

of extricating oneself from the long thong binding.

The Minnesota - Wisconsin *SKI NEWS* published an article about the first annual Twin City Downhill and Slalom Championships at Buck Hill on February 13, 1955. There were nearly 50 racers competing for titles in the women's and men's class, A, B, and C divisions. The following description of the race is quite remarkable:

The downhill was run first over a course nearly ½ mile long made quite tricky with icy conditions, ruts, narrow trail through heavy brush and a treacherous jump. The spills were quite frequent and spectacular. Nearly 1/3 of the racers fell at some point on the course. The toughest part to handle was a sharp pull-out at the bottom of the icy headwall. It was immediately followed by a huge mogul flanked on either side by large oak trees. If the racer failed to run this part of the course correctly, he was faced with another tree directly in his path. Many of the competitors flew fifty feet off the treacherous jump (yes, that's what it said). This part of the course caused more speculation and experimentation than any portion of the course set by the racing council.

There was hardly a racer that was not nervous at the start and many claimed they would "walk down" the course rather than hit the bump wide open. Form was sacrificed for stability as the racers attained speeds of 40 mph plus. Carol Bjorn was the winner of the women's division with John Hansen winning class A, Bob Tengdin class B and Gil Silverman class C.

The slalom was tricky and very fast. Only one run was held because a course setter got badly hurt by a spike on the tip of the slalom pole and after that had been taken care of it was too late to have another run. Nancy MacGibbon was the winner of the women's slalom and John Hansen won the men's slalom in class A.

I remember a particularly exciting day in February of 1955 when Chuck proposed to me on the hill, of course. Maybe it happened on Nancy's Folly! Buck Hill had been incorporated in September of 1954 and we were married one year later.

That first year we installed a 1,000 ft. rope tow that was powered by a Ford gasoline

Mr. and Mrs. Chuck Stone
September 24, 1955

engine. Chuck was acutely aware of how cold our winters could be and of course it was imperative that our one and only rope tow started in the morning when the skiers arrived. He was very concerned the Ford engine would freeze up on cold nights. To solve that problem Chuck spent some very frigid nights on top of the hill in the non-insulated tow house with a tiny space heater. He would start the engine every half hour or so to keep it in top operating condition.

Another race the following year was covered in the *Minneapolis Star Journal* on February 12, 1956 titled **Central Ski Here Sunday**:

> Duluth entries are a heavy favorite Sunday in the Central United States Ski Association (CUSSA) four-man downhill and slalom championships at Buck Hill, 10 miles south of Minneapolis on highway 65. The competition is the first CUSSA sanctioned racing event in the Twin Cities in 10 years. Downhill events are slated for 11:00 a.m. and slalom 1:30 p.m. Total time of each four -man team is added together to determine winners. The Buck Hill Club will enter three men's teams and one women's unit. No 1 team is composed of Fred Lang, John Hansen, Tom Vitala and Bob Tengdin. Pat Gleason, Carol Bjorn, Nancy Stone and Trudy Peet make up the women's foursome. Duluth will be represented by at least three teams which will include Ivan Iverson and the Slotness brothers.

Pat Gleason, a very accomplished and enthusiastic racer wrote an article for the *Mid-West Skier* on October 15, 1956 which summed up the racing in the Twin Cities to date. She mentioned the success of the previous winter's four-man team championships and the fact that they would be held again this coming winter season in 1957. Pat continued, "The area at Buck Hill is well suited for both beginning and advanced skiers. The beginners have a tow and hill especially designed for them and more experienced skiers will find a hill as challenging as anything in the Midwest. Mr. and Mrs. Chuck Stone own and operate Buck Hill and are both avid skiers. Chuck has always been most willing to let his area be used for an occasional Sunday race, a rare thing among operators of commercial areas. I'm sure that all racers are most grateful to him for this attitude. The club hopes that it will be able to further its development

1959-1960 brochure cover, designed by Marea Campbell.

of racing through its activities."

The winter seasons of 1954-55 and 1955-56 were very lean years in terms of corporate income, even though the total snow depth was only slightly below the Minneapolis average. Even a natural snowfall of 8 inches tends to become worn away very quickly with even a modest amount of skiers. The ski area was operating with only one tow and on weekends only.

The seasons of 1956-61 were extremely poor snow years and the area operated a grand total of only six days during the combined four winter seasons. The lift rate at that time was $2 a day. Believe it or not, when we went into the ski business, it simply did not occur to us that some years there might not be enough snow to operate the ski area. However, we soon became confronted with this reality. We probably should have known better because, in the 1930's for example, there were quite a few years without any snow at all or rain too for that matter. Although the snow situation was terrible in Minnesota, Aspen had plenty, and we managed a few trips to Colorado when the action was quiet at Buck Hill!

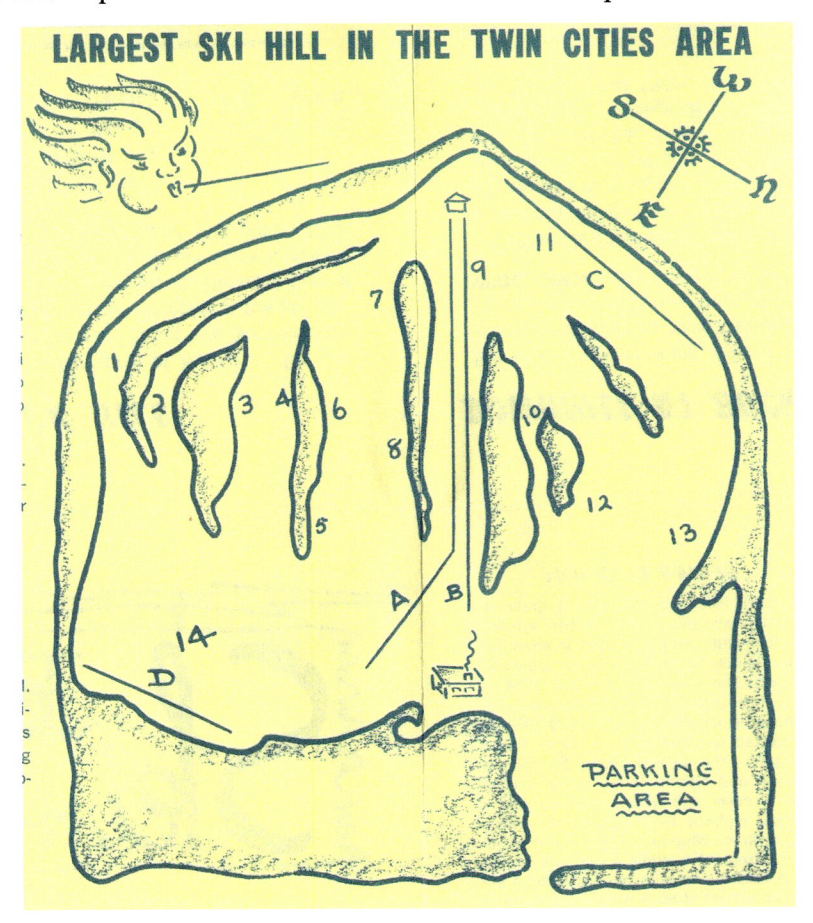

First Trail Map. (1. Way Around, 2. Glen's Glen,
3. Bell Slalom, 4. Stone's Throw, 5. Lindley's Race Trail, 6. Jari Gulch, 7. Chute,
8. Nancy's Folly, 9. SumSchuss, 10. Bob's Bump, 11. North Side,
12. Mrs. Fostah's Fancy)

Although the snowfall during the late 1950's was disappointing, the prospects for the ski business still looked promising. According to a 1958 *Minneapolis Star Tribune* survey of Minnesota Living, five percent of all urban Minnesota men participated in skiing and approximately half as many women skied. Based on population figures at that time it meant there were about 45,000 skiers in the

Twin Cities area. *Skiing Magazine* reported in 1958 that skiing was considered one of the fastest growing sports in America, and estimated there were a total of three and a half million skiers in the whole country. By contrast, in 2013 there were approximately 65 million skiers and snowboarders in the United States. We were confident that if we could just have reliable snow, Buck Hill was bound to be successful.

Lunch time in the 60's. Cable bindings are in!

At that time, Buck Hill's assets consisted of 2 rope tows – a 1,000 ft. and a 1,200 ft. powered by 2 Caterpillar 140 HP diesel engines. Our chalet was 1,020 square feet and we also owned a small Oliver Crawler Tractor for hill maintenance. In the summer of 1955, we added two more rope tows in order to provide easier terrain for beginners and we needed to make more capital investments but Buck Hill was frightfully under financed. Since the lease had been extended to 1982, it was

1961-1962 season, new T-Bar.

decided that it was definitely time to raise some money for our needed capital improvements. Chuck and Walter Bush drafted a prospectus dated May 14, 1959. Buck Hill, Inc. was authorized to issue 100,000 additional shares of common stock at $1 a share. The goal was to use the proceeds to fund snowmaking equipment ($35,000), an addition to the chalet ($20,00), a T-Bar ($20,000), a Sno-Cat ($5,000) and other miscellaneous items. The chalet addition would include additional rental space and equipment, a ski patrol room and two bathrooms. Other improvements included $500 to be spent on re-grading the parking lot and enlarging its capacity from 300 to 500 cars.

Approximately 50,000 shares of stock were sold which was enough to start the new projects. We were overjoyed to welcome 35 new shareholders! Most of the investors were avid skiers and received a 10-year season pass for every 700 shares that they purchased. However, it immediately became apparent that we underestimated the capital needed to include the T-Bar and it was necessary to find another source of revenue. Harrison Freeman put together a small group of

his friends including, Oz Wyatt, Gordon Ellebe, and himself called FEW Enterprises.
They financed a loan of $11,000 and the T-Bar construction was underway. The group received 50 cents on every lift ticket sold. The lift was paid for in a year and the investors received a 25% gain on their investment.

Duncan Grandin in the rental shop mounting bindings.

Over the years, the success of Buck Hill can be attributed in large part to the hard work and dedication of many many loyal employees. This was especially true in the 1950's and 1960's when we were starting the business and conditions and equipment were somewhat primitive. There were often times when the unexpected happened, such as a rope needing to be spliced immediately, and it was never at a convenient time. It could be -10 degrees and it had to be done with bare hands so there was always a little bonfire nearby to thaw the hands. Chuck was a hands-on manager and never asked an employee to do a job that he would not do himself. Often Chuck did the splicing, but many others did as well. Their shift may have ended, but they would willingly stay to help as long as it took to finish the job without any complaints.

One of the most time consuming and unsavory jobs was digging up frozen, leaking underground snowmaking pipes. First, the system had to be drained and then the ground had to be thawed in order to get to the pipe. Next, a new piece of pipe had to be welded in place and then reburied with hopes that it would hold when the system was started up again. These were hard-working young men who really cared about the success of Buck Hill. We were truly blessed and grateful for these early, enthusiastic employees.

Laced boots, colorful outfits and natural snow, 1963.

THE SIXTIES

*Building of 35W, Artificial Snow, New T-Bar,
New Manager Stuart Campbell, Summer Business,
Hall Chairlift, Acquiring Powder Ridge, Ron Greely,
Snowcraft J-Bar, Buck Hill Racing Team, Ladies Day,
Wind Chill, Miner-Denver Chairlift, The Arrival of
Erich Sailer*

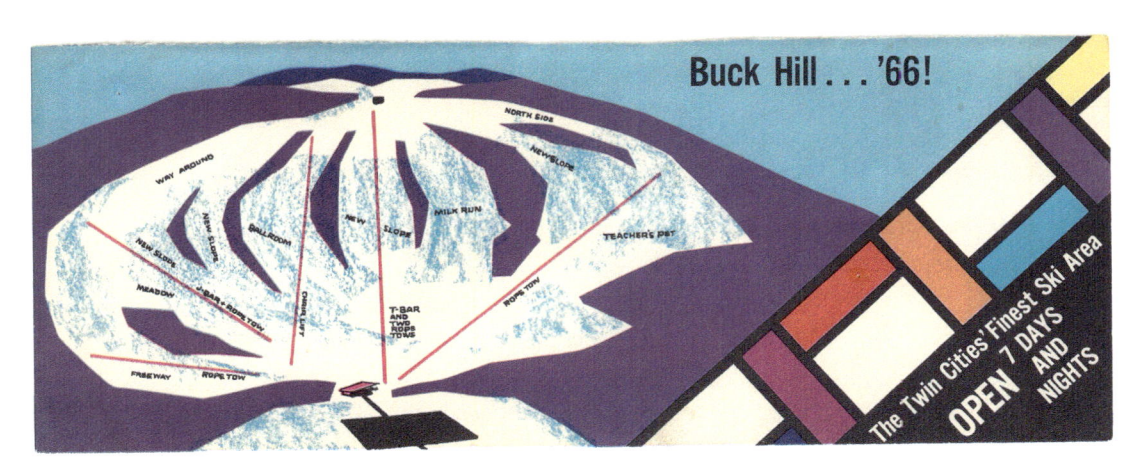

*The 1966-1967 winter season brought a new double chair lift to add to the
one J-Bar, five rope tows, and three new runs to be named by skiers.*

Meanwhile the farm land around Buck Hill began to be developed, slowly at first and then more rapidly. The towns of Lakeville and Burnsville began to grow as well. Burnsville did not officially become a city until 1987, 33 years after Buck Hill was started. Along with this growth came many new laws and regulations which made doing business much more difficult, and more expensive as well. We no longer borrowed tools from the local farmers or went down the road to buy dynamite! At the end of the 50's, the real estate taxes were $183.05 on twice as much acreage than we have today, compared to 2015, when the real estate taxes were $80,000!

A new beginners rope tow.

The Annual Shareholders meeting was held December 1, 1960. Officers were Charles Stone President, Stuart Campbell Vice President, Walter Bush Jr. Secretary, and Nancy Stone Treasurer. Theodore Stark and Co were appointed accountants for the corporation. Article III of the by-laws was amended to "no less than three and no more than seven directors. A loan from the First National Bank was secured for $5,000.

While implementing the new improvements, we were notified by the Minnesota Highway Department that plans were under way to construct an interstate to replace Highway 65. Chuck contacted the highway department many times but he was given the "run around" and could not get any definite answers to specific questions. He was especially concerned about the drainage problems that might, and eventually did occur.

On June 6, 1961, Chuck wrote a letter to the Minnesota State Highway Department:

> The reason I am writing you is that they are planning a service road in front of the ski area and I would like to know the definite construction limits of this road so as not to incur any great deal of expense on the states part or, naturally on our own. We are involved in a major construction project at the area and much has been slated for the land fairly close to the highway.

I cannot emphasize enough how much of a negative impact the construction of Interstate 35W had on Buck Hill at the time. Our lease with Grace Whittier also included 26 acres on the east side of the highway adjacent to Crystal Lake and we had talked of plans for a summer camp in the future. We had been paying taxes on those 26 acres for 6 years. Grace also had potential plans for her property on the lake which included a hotel with a view of the lake to the east and the ski area to the west. It would have been a fantastic addition to Burnsville, but 35W put an end to that particular vision.

Some of the problems we had to face at the time included a lost ski trail which of course was irreplaceable, lack of adequate drainage which caused serious flooding, and costly engineering as a new lift had to be redesigned. We had also requested an underpass or an overpass for access to Crystal Lake, which was denied. In addition, wind erosion and aesthetic problems arose on our eastern border due to the removal of trees and a wooded setting. The drainage issue, as Chuck predicted, proved to be a major problem, causing considerable havoc, which took over six years to resolve.

Of course, the biggest challenge we faced in operating Buck Hill was the reliance on natural snow. It soon became evident that relying on natural snowfalls was a detriment to the success of any ski area and that was especially true for the smaller areas in the Midwest like Buck Hill. These were the very early days of snowmaking and its implementation was about to revolutionize the industry.

Chuck wrote about early snowmaking:

The 50's and 60's were tremendous growth years for the ski business and literally hundreds of ski areas were built across Canada and the United States. The number of skier visits were increasing from 10-15% per year and the ski areas were meeting this demand with new resorts. The 1960 Olympics at Squaw Valley fueled these interests as some United States ski areas received world recognition. High schools and colleges across the country organized ski teams and the sport received local recognition. In the mid 1950s snow making was in its very early stages. It was soon developed commercially which eliminated some of the reliance on Mother Nature, and areas were built as far south as North Carolina, Virginia and southern New Mexico.

Artificial snow is made by combining compressed air and water in air temperatures below 32 degrees Fahrenheit. This is done at

Snowmaker Dennis Rohrer, unknown person, and Gordy Anderson skiing by.

a ski area by running one pipe from a water supply and one from a compressed air supply along the sides of the trails. At various intervals along these pipes, hydrants are installed to transfer the water and compressed air by flexible tubing to a nozzle similar to one used in watering golf courses and irrigation systems. It is here that the compressed air and water meet. The water under pressure (approximately 20 gallons per minute, per nozzle) as it leaves the nozzle is met by the compressed air (100 cubic feet per minute, per nozzle) which, as it expands and cools, rapidly freezes and crystalizes the water and it falls as snow. This process is an application of the Venturi principle.

On April 11, 1961, we were able to hire Stuart Campbell as the new general manager. Stuart's wife, Ginny, was also very involved at the ski area. Ginny became an all around assistant to Stuart in almost every department. She helped Sis Grogan and Judy Alm with the ladies' day programs and lent a hand in the kitchen and ticket office when needed. Buck Hill's famous donuts were added to the menu in the cafeteria at this time and they proved to be very popular. The Campbell's noticed that the enticing aroma caused skiers to linger in the chalet a bit longer and therefore kept the slopes a little less crowded. Ginny a very talented artist designed and painted many of the signs around the area. Another valuable employee in those days was Betty Wallien, whom Stuart called a "Jackie of all Trades."

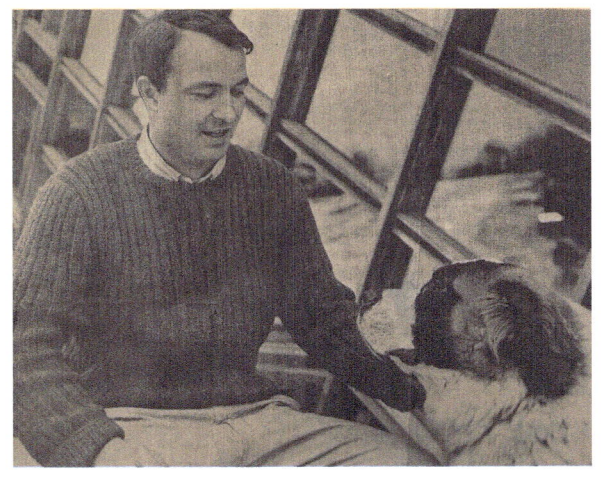

Manager Stuart Campbell of Buck Hill with his dog Brandy. Sun Suburbanite, Dec. 1965

Chuck worked for the Charles W. Stone Company as a salesman and held that position all of his life. Of course he also spent every possible free moment working at Buck Hill. He was definitely a "hands on executive" and was involved in all aspects of running Buck Hill including, from time to time, using heavy machinery. One time, Chuck was working with a back hoe to help prepare the slopes for the installation of some snowmaking pipes but on this occasion, things didn't go exactly as planned. The following excerpt is from a letter from ATT to its Plant Superintendent in Chicago. This letter describes Chuck's folly best:

One of the things Buck Hill had planned at the time, but did not mention to our people, was the placing of a series of pipes from the lodge up the slopes for use in *watering the slopes and freezing them for better skiing* (clearly, he was not a fan of the sport). The route of the pipes would take them directly over our cable as can be seen from the attached sketch. On Sunday, October 15, 1961, with no notification to the telephone company, trenching was done down the ski slopes of the ski slide. At approximately 2:25 P.M. on that date our cable was struck by a back hoe mounted on a tractor. The tractor was being driven by Mr. Charles W. Stone, Jr., President of Buck Hill, Inc.

The incident cost us $379.79 and yes, we did get snowmaking in that year, installing 7,200 feet of aluminum pipe.

We were all very excited in anticipation of the upcoming winter season of 1961-1962. To ensure dependable skiing, snowmaking machines had been installed and at least 3 slopes were covered throughout the winter. We had a license from Larchmont Engineering to use their method to make snow. The new electric compressors made it possible for us to make 1400 cubic feet of snow per minute. The runs for beginners, intermediate and experts varied in length from 700 ft. to 3,000 ft. with a 313 ft. vertical drop. They were served by a $25,000 Hall high-speed T-Bar and 4 electrically powered rope tows. Of course it didn't occur to us at the

Checking out the fall line; mid 1960's

time that looming ahead would be those mid to late Novembers when it would not be cold enough to make snow. An early start is a prerequisite for a banner year.

The winter season of 1961-1962 was the first winter that we operated the area straight through for 85 days and 65 nights and had 14,703 skiers. This was only possible because of the installation of the artificial snowmaking system. That

Notice that lace boots are still in style!

first snowmaking season our gross receipts rose from $699.00 the previous season to $64,804 in 1962. In June of 1962, Chuck wrote to the shareholders about the successful season and added, "Last fall after an all night work session, the day before we opened the area the last T-bar was bolted to the wire rope at 7:30 A.M. and the first person to ride was a paying customer."

There isn't any question that snowmaking was the technology that revolutionized the ski business. I do not know where Buck Hill would be today without it. It might have become a housing development or perhaps a gravel pit (which is what Grace Whittier often said). There has not been one winter, since that first season, that Buck Hill has

not depended on snowmaking even in years with abundant snowfalls. The first snowmaking machines were incredibly energy intensive but energy back then didn't cost much. One of the guns in the early days might consume 95KW of electrical energy. Today a modern gun uses 4.5KW.

Buck Hill in 1962

Buck Hill continued to invest in the latest snowmaking technology and its ability to quickly and completely blanket the hill with snow increased tremendously. For instance, in 1962 Buck Hill had 15 snow guns which produced 20 gallons of snow per minute. By 2015 it owned 150 snow guns, mostly Areco, made in Sweden, and TechnoAlpin, made in Italy, which were capable of producing 2,700 gallons of snow per minute. This updated system resulted in Buck Hill being able to open the entire ski area in only three days if the temperature was right.

Of course having enough snow in the winter was not the only concern we had. Another major concern for anyone in the ski business was what to do in the off season so that those months could become productive for the business, rather

than a detriment. We embarked on our first summer business in 1962 with a Sky Ride. We had special chairs made that could be attached to the T-Bar, so that customers could ride to the top of Buck Hill for a picnic or a hike down. There was a spectacular view of the Minneapolis sky line and all the surrounding area which was mostly farmland. Buck Hill had a small restaurant in the chalet where one could get a

New T-Bar, 1962

box lunch to take to the top. Unfortunately, the financial results of the summers of 1962 and 1963 showed far less income than we had hoped for.

1962	Sky Ride	3,758 rides at 50 cents	$1,879.00
	Restaurant		$1,336.00
	Gift Shop		$350.00
	Total		$3,565.00
1963	Sky Ride	4,352 rides at 50 cents	$2,176.00
	Restaurant		$1,411.00
	Gift Shop		$369.00
	Stirrup Club		$2,700.00
	Total		$6,656.00

In summer of 1962, Ben Kern wrote about the Sky Ride in the *Minneapolis Morning Tribune*:

Buck Hill offers summer rides: Now you can drive 20 miles south of downtown Minneapolis on Highways 35W and 65M, ride a chair to the top of a high hill, turn around and see downtown Minneapolis. You can see similar distances in other directions. The chair ride is part of an answer to a problem besetting Buck Hill, Inc. as it does quite a few other Upper Midwest ski areas – lack of summer revenue. Chuck Stone, Buck Hill's President, said the area had a good season last winter but that it wants to become self-supporting year round before it "plunges" ahead into further expansion. He is in the machine tool business and did an ingenious job of fitting the T-Bar lift with summertime chairs. Stuart Campbell, Buck Hill's full-time manager, showed me the painted foot prints on which to stand while waiting for a chair. You just stand there and fold into it when it comes along. It swings a little and that makes it more fun. There is nothing like a chair for riding up hill.

Buck Hill Accountant, Rip West, giving his daughter Sue a lift at Powder Ridge.

In the fall of 1962, a new ski newspaper *The Buck Hill Express* would cover the skiing news at Buck Hill. Editor in Chief was Bruce Abbe. He was also Ski School Director at Powder Ridge. In addition, Abbe edited the Powder Ridge ski newspaper, the famous *Powder Ridge Gazette*.

In the summer of 1963, we had

horseback riding through the American Stirrup Club, which was owned and operated by Stuart (Bootie) Gordon. Although these summer activities were not the answer to a viable off season business, it was a start. The Sky Ride did not open the next season due to the construction on Highway 35W. That summer we also brought on our new accountant and good friend, David (Rip) West, a founder of Johnson, West and Co., an accounting firm in St. Paul.

The shareholders were informed of the coming season: "Starting our Tenth season of operation, Buck Hill has just completed a $45,000 refurbishing plan including the addition of a unique Sto-Craft J-Bar lift and a new beginners slope which brings the total number of ski runs to 11. The new beginner's area called "The Meadow," will be serviced by the J-Bar as well as a 900- ft double rope tow.

1963 Aerial View of Buck Hill. Notice the entrance to Hwy 65 and the lack of neighbors.

Stuart reminded me of a memorable incident while installing the J-Bar. It was a beautiful fall day and he had driven up the hill in his inherited, old, brown, Plymouth station wagon to bring tools and supplies to the job site and he parked just below the crest of the hill. Stuart joined the other workers and soon they decided to break for lunch. Surprise! The car was not where he had left it but it was quickly spotted half way down the hill and had hit a stump. Gratefully, he opened the front door and lo and behold the engine was in the front seat!

Gunpowder at Powder Ridge, 1965

I remember some trips to St. Cloud in the summer of 1964 to meet with Ken and Midge Dean and some of the other investors in the Powder Ridge Ski Area. We knew the Dean's from ski racing days. Chuck was very interested in buying the area if it could be purchased for the right price. Powder Ridge was developed in the early 1950's by a group of St. Cloud area investors. In 1956, the first rope tow was installed and soon replaced with a double rope and a small chalet was built. In 1960, the first Larchmount snow-making system in the Midwest was installed to ensure good snow for skiing. The next few years were a struggle for the area and it collapsed in 1964.

From Powder Ridge Ski Area History by Janet Robinson:

High up, but not on the very peak of the only hill in the entire area of Maine Prairie, lived Elmer and Emma (Swisher) Eaton. They were early settlers and lived their entire lives in the Kimball area. Emma died in 1941 and Elmer in 1944. Their cozy little homestead consisted of their low, unpainted house with a rain barrel standing at the corner near the only door. There was a clothesline and fenced-in garden area to the south, a long building with a cow barn at the other end, combination granary, tool shed, and workshop in the middle, and horse barn at the other end, east of the house. On the top of the hill and around to the west was a pasture with trees. This homestead became known to their grandchildren as "Grandpa's Hill." This hill later became known as Powder Ridge Ski Resort.

Like Buck Hill, Powder Ridge was built in a rural area, surrounded by farms as far as you could see. According to the Minnesota Geological Survey, Powder Ridge was formed 15,000 years ago as part of the Lake Superior lobe of the Wisconsin glacial period. It is a terminal moraine (at the end of a glacier), just like Buck Hill. As the glacier melted, it left behind a load of dirt and rocks. Chuck was interested in acquiring the ski area. Since it was only about 60 miles from the Twin Cities it would be easy to manage both areas. Both of us were attracted to it because of the beautiful setting and also its low key and casual atmosphere. It reminded us of Buck Hill. Chuck bought Powder Ridge for $5,000 in bankruptcy court and sold it to Buck Hill, Inc. for the same amount.

We went right to work making some improvements at Powder Ridge. The co-managers at the area were Jim Caauwe and John Bristol. Buck Hill Corporation, now comprised of both Buck Hill and Powder Ridge, had 7

Early Powder Ridge brochure, late 1950's.

full time employees and a seasonal staff of 126. Both areas had snow making and Buck Hill had recently added more night skiing.

At Powder Ridge, a bar called The Gesundheit Room was added that served bratwurst and 3.2 beer. The lounge featured the music of Terry LaPanta singing, blowing kazoo and harmonica, strumming a guitar and banging a tambourine! The long time employee and bar

Front entrance to Hwy 65 in 1963.

manager, Ed Rahe, always believed that the secret to the bratwurst was its source, the Knaus' Sausage House in nearby Kimball, Minnesota.

By 1964, Buck Hill was firmly established and even attracted attention from a reporter, Bob Cary, of the *Chicago Daily News*. The following is an excerpt from his article from Jan. 4, 1964:

> Dartmouth College, in New England, is over a thousand miles from Minneapolis and St. Paul, but the school must be given credit for an "assist" when anyone mentions construction of the Twin Cities ski area at Buck Hill.
>
> When Minneapolis student, Chuck Stone, graduated from Dartmouth a dozen years ago he came home looking for some place to pursue his newly-developed sport.
>
> The spot he picked was Buck Hill, five miles south of the cities, the highest elevation in the (metro) area. He rounded up some cash, and formed a corporation.

Meanwhile at Buck Hill, we spent the summer and fall of 1965 preparing some new runs and installing a Hall double chair lift. This was an exciting event and it was very well received even before the season opened. The new lift, which cost in excess of $50,000, had 51 chairs with safety bars and increased the hill's capacity by more than 1,200 skiers per hour. Along with the new lift, came two new runs which originated from the top of the hill.

Installing the Bullwheel for the new Hall Double Chair Lift.

The Milk Run was for experts and Crossroads for intermediates. Three tons of steel were raised in positioning a giant, 10-foot diameter bull wheel at the foot of the lift. Geared to a 50-horsepower electric motor, the bull wheel powered the chairs around the pivot and up the hill. More than a half mile of 1-1/8 inch carrying cable was used in constructing the lift. Buck Hill now had 1 chairlift, 1 T-bar, 1 J-bar and 5 rope tows.

These improvements were also mentioned in an article by Ben Kern in the *Minneapolis Tribune*. In the same article, other ski areas' improvements were also mentioned across the Midwest. Pine Bend Ski Area owner, Oscar Cyr, was so busy with the business that he had not even been on skis that season! The article also described how Pine Bend had turned away 500 skiers in one day due to capacity issues.

The new J-Bar; notice Hwy 65.

In the early 1960's there was a blizzard of new skiers due to the roving ski schools that were organized at that time and were very popular. Roving ski schools were independently owned and took their skier students on buses to different ski areas during the winter. They were always welcome at Buck Hill and Powder Ridge. Some thank-you notes Chuck had written to the owners included the following (and I think there were others): Paul Mascoti of Eskimo Ski School, Otto Hollaus of Otto Hollaus Ski School, Bill and Frannie Owen and Jim and Nancy Countryman* of Skijammers' Ski School, Jerry Schiep of Tyrol Ski school, Glen Pfaff of Hoigaards' Ski School, Charles Witt of Ski-Bo Club, Earl Mosiman of Tatra Ski School and William Horgan of Blizzard Ski Club. There was also the Traveling Ski School owned by Tim Johnson which catered to the Northfield area.

The Tonkawood Ski School was a fine example of a program that catered to very young skiers. The age requirements were three and up. This school was started in 1967 by Ellie Crosby and Patty Dickey. After going to different ski areas in the early years, the school had been going to Powder Ridge since the '84-'85 winter season and was still going strong in 2015. Co-directors were Ellie Crosby and Nancy Bizzano and they gave the small children a very positive introduction to the great sport of skiing. I am sorry if I left some schools out but please know we were grateful to have your business.

Kathy Lingo, a loyal Buck Hill skier, wrote about her treasured memories of skiing at Buck Hill in the 60s:

> I loved skiing there. I had an old pair of wooden skis with leather bindings and old square toed leather boots. I must have inherited them from a family member because no one had skis like that. But I learned to do snowplow turns, and gradually struggled down the hill. The snow was constantly changing, sometimes slushy, and sometimes slick and icy. You never knew how the conditions would be. The base was not always very deep and you had to be careful for rocks and dirt that could be showing, especially in the spring. The tows were scary at first until you got used to them. The hill seemed so high that it felt like a mountain and the view was very pretty. But I loved skiing there no matter how many times I fell, and it was often. It wasn't as crowded later as it grew in popularity. When we skied in the evening, it was so beautiful and peaceful and we were never cold. The snow almost seemed better at night – firmer but not so icy. Skiing was a very fun sport and winter became my favorite season as I looked forward to skiing from April until December. Buck Hill was and still is a great fun spot.

Some very valuable employees in those years, as best we can recall (remember that was over 50 years ago) were crucial in providing excellent skiing for our guests. George Lamphere headed up the snow making crew with Bill Bottineau, Geno Peterson, Jerry Brueggen and others. Lyle B. Olson was in charge of grooming and he also owned a sod company which employed some of these men in the off season, which worked out very well. The friendly lift operators were Dennis Caauwe, Dan Gustafson, Wally Day and many others. Our friend Tony Sellwood began taking on some of our advertising at this time and some of his drawings won prestigious awards.

Chuck and Alex Petri discussing some events in the fireplace room.

Speaking of Geno Peterson, in 1966 the 14-

year old boy wandered over from the back of the hill where he lived to apply for a job. His first assignment was picking up trash in the parking lot between shifts. For a few short years the area was closed from 4:30-7:00 P.M. Geno did just about everything at one time or another at the area and he was an excellent carpenter. Early on he made snow with George Lamphere and others. He was a lift operator running rope tows, a T-Bar, J-Bar and chairlifts, and helped install them too. He assisted Chuck in splicing ropes and remembered how Chuck would have his gloves on strings so he wouldn't loose them. Geno recalled the temperatures on those occasions being about forty below zero (or so it seemed). He had his own home building business in the off season.

Some other loyal employees in those years were Steve Bauer, Dick Lempke, Tom Hummel, Dave Milan, John Frieges and Jack Olson, alias Elvis and Santa. Sue McClish was one of the kitchen workers, and a romance evolved and Sue married Geno Peterson.

In the winter of 1964-1965 Buck Hill offered a "SUNDAY EVENING SPECIAL:"

Ski from 4: P.M. to 5: P.M, then enjoy
a Sunday supper of pancakes.
Entertainment by the Riverboat Ramblers*
And return to the slopes from 7:PM. to 10:PM.

Steve Peer, leader of the Riverboat Ramblers, soon left Minnesota for Aspen and we saw them performing at the base of Little Nell in the 80s. They were as entertaining there as they had been at Buck Hill.

The winter of 1964-1965 was a good season. In terms of skier days, Buck Hill was the largest ski area in the state of Minnesota. However, we were still having problems with drainage issues caused by I-35W and still negotiating with the Minnesota Highway Department to find a reasonable solution. In 1965, Walter Bush wrote to the department: "Unless we are able to reach some satisfactory solution, apparently the only method of settlement would be legal in nature, as the officers of Buck Hill feel a responsibility to the shareholders to protect the very valuable assets of the corporation."

A flooded parking lot, 1965

During this time, we were

Skijammers Visit Powder Ridge

The "Skijammers" Ski Club of Wayzata, 15 strong invaded Powder Ridge recently to hold an instructor's clinic. They were kind enough to pose for our cameraman.
We're proud to introduce them to you. Pictured on the left from L. to

R. are: Chuck Witt, Franny Owen, director, Nancy Countryman, Sue King-man, Gil Silverman, Paul Konsterlie, Don Burris and Ron Weisner.
On the right, L. to R. are: Dick Reid, Jim Countryman, director, Hans Riefer, Susie Snyder, Wally May, Jim Windy and Bill Ackerman.

December, 1965

able to temporarily solve the parking problem and the drainage issue from the construction of 35W by using the church parking lot across the road and parking in the southbound lane of the freeway under construction. However, on February 25,1965 flooding problems began again after a mild rain and warm spell. The parking lot became flooded and it was impossible to park cars. With the approval of the highway department we had to lay a hose over the heavily trafficked, southbound lane of the freeway and pump into the median stretch. This solution alleviated the problem temporarily and we were able to stay open until April 7th that year. Meanwhile, at the bottom of the hill, the garage and pump house were completely under water adding considerable damage and expense.

It is noteworthy that in the 50's and 60's, and even the 70's, skiing in general received a lot of attention from the local press. I imagine that was because the sport was growing so rapidly and there were consistently new happenings and improvements at the ski areas. Afton Alps opened in 1963 and Welsh Village opened in 1965. Buck Hill was considered the elite of the metro ski areas by the *Sun Suburbanite* in 1965. It made mention of our ability to handle thousands of skiers a day and it also pointed out that we had the most modern equipment available. Ralph Thornton's column, **Ski Country**, is an example of the award winning coverage of skiing provided by *The Minneapolis Star and Tribune*. The United States Ski Association, Central Division, in 1967, honored Thornton as "Ski Writer of the Year."

Alex Petri, Ski School Director, 1963.
Hard to choose between skiing and golf!

Ski-Nuz

VOLUME II, NO. 1 — BUCK HILL — OCTOBER, 1966

WHETHER IT SNOWS OR NOT WE'LL BE SKIING

Linnea Peterson Rowe remembered what it was like to ski at Buck Hill in the mid sixties. Alex Petri was Buck Hill's ski school director. He rented a room from Linneas' family and often gave Linnea and her brothers days of skiing that they always looked forward to:

> Our equipment was nothing special. My dad bought me a used pair of skis that had a clip to snap my boots in. It didn't matter that everyone else had the "step-in" bindings, I was just happy to be there. It was always a challenge to get the lace up boots just right. Our favorite run was to take the T-Bar up to the top and then we would ski around the back to the hill farthest south. We would pretend we were in the mountains and it was fun to look down on what we called "the little village" which was the trailer home park. The chair lift was always fun as we tried to do something fancy getting on and off the lift. We were trying to catch the eye of the cute boys running the lift....9th grade silliness.

The Ski-Nuz October 1966 issue, Buck Hill's in-house newspaper, featured some important happenings at both areas. First and foremost, Powder Ridge gained a new general manager, Ron Greely, who was a Kimball native. Ron had extensive managerial experience and was the owner of a chain of successful drive-in theatres. The beginners' area of the hill was re-graded and a new double rope tow was installed. New snowmaking equipment was also installed and there was night skiing twice a week on Wednesday and Friday nights.

Ron Greely, new general manager at Powder Ridge.

Meanwhile at Buck Hill, night skiing had become very popular with all ages seven nights a week until 10:00 p.m. Night skiing has always seemed to be more pleasurable since 99% of the time there is no wind and also, with sun glares gone, surface lumps and contours are more easily distinguished under the lights. Snow conditions are often above par since the sun's rays have disappeared and surface cooling is in effect. Fortunately, these conditions also contributed to the popularity of night racing. Many local ski teams practiced at night including the Buck Hill Ski Team. We continued to get some attention from the local press and Chuck was never shy about offering his insights. In a *Minneapolis Star Tribune* article by Dwayne Netland, Chuck was quoted as saying "Being in the ski business is like holding a tiger by the tail. You've got to keep improving the facilities or fall by the wayside."

In a December 23, 1966 *Star Tribune* article by Ben Kern he reported on our snow-making ability:

> The current cold snap was the nicest Christmas present the snow-making ski areas around the Twin Cities could get. The distant lights of the city are beautiful from the top of Buck Hill at night. The specks of color from the far away neons gave the star speckled panorama a Christmas look. When I skied at Buck Hill, mild weather had prevented snow-making for five nights and the temperature was above freezing yet the 3 runs were well covered with a heavy man made base.

In the fall of 1966, a significant addition was the formation of the Buck Hill Junior Alpine Ski Racing Team. Walter Huestis was the first coach and there were 12 boys on the team. Martha Hustad and Buzz Bainbridge Jr. were also coaches in those early years. The junior racers competed in the fledging USSA Central Division Region 1 races. Ralph Thornton wrote about the progress of the team in the *Minneapolis Star* in the fall of 1967:

The first Olympic medalist to head a Minnesota Ski School arrived at Buck Hill this week. Within hours after his arrival, Tony Spiss, a St. Anton, Austria native and former Austrian champion had introduced the Buck Hill junior racing

The first Powder Ridge brochure.

team to European training methods.

Spiss left Buck Hill after two seasons at the area. Erich Sailer came to Buck Hill in 1969 and took the team to a whole new level. More information on the history of the ski team is found in the ski team section of this book.

There is no doubt that the success of Buck Hill's Junior Racing program has contributed significantly to the recognition we have received all over the country and internationally as well. Chuck and I have ridden up chairlifts in the east and west with people who have heard of Buck Hill because of our racing program. Erich was to become one of the most successful junior alpine coaches in the entire country.

Buck Hill has always been very proud of its ski patrol. It had an exceptional

Chuck clowning around at Buck Hill winter carnival.

Stoney and Polly Stone deciding which run to take at Powder Ridge.

John Bristol helping Jessica learn to ski at Powder Ridge.

Cindy and Chuckie at the Winter Carnival, 1966.

beginning and continues to excel to this day. Our first patrol director Jerry Fredrickson, was named outstanding ski patrolman of the year in 1967 for the western region of the United States Ski Association, which included the Rocky Mountain area. The Buck Hill Ski Patrol was singled out as the number one ski patrol in the Midwest by the CUSSA's Central Division. Over the years, it has continued to win many awards. The performance of the ski patrol has always been of the utmost importance to Buck Hill.

Starting in the mid 60's we always had a spring carnival at both ski areas. The idea may have come from Chuck's memories of the very traditional winter carnivals at Dartmouth which was the first college to have a winter carnival back in 1910.

In a 1967 *Star Tribune* article Ben Kern described the Powder Ridge carnival:

At Powder Ridge, former slalom man and president of the Buck Hill corporation (Chuck Stone) which owns Powder Ridge was running the Powder Ridge Carnival and enjoying it – announcing races, leading the costume parade in a clown suit and putting the kids through an obstacle course. With Chuck at Powder Ridge was his wife Nancy who once raced in the Olympic tryouts at Sun Valley. Their son, Chuckie 11, and daughter, Cindy 9, were junior racers in the carnival. Cindy in a bunny suit handed out candy eggs.

Outside Crew, 1968. Back: Unknown, Fred Peterson, Lyle Boyer, Unknown, Unknown, Bob Caauwe, Unknown, Unknown. Front: Steve Bauer, Clark Johnson, Lynne Throne, Dennis Rohrer, Terry Young, Unknown, Unknown, and Brandy the St. Bernard.

I did do a little racing at Sun Valley, but I am so sorry to say not in the Olympic try-outs.

One fond memory I have of Buck Hill happened in the summer of 1967 and involved Jim Caauwe who, at the time, was our outside operations manager. At the very bottom of the hill there was a large pile of brush from clearing the trails. One day Jim heard some whimpering from the brush and upon investigating further he found a mother Samoyed and her litter of darling little white puppies. The mother had wandered on to the hill and fell in love with Stuart Gordon's German Shepard. The owner finally claimed his dog but gave us one puppy that we named Stoney. If it was a very slow day on the hill we would let him follow us up under the chair and then he ran beside us when we skied down. Stoney stayed with us for 15 years!

Jim's brother, Bob Caauwe, was instrumental in finding lift operators at Lakeville High School. Of course, lift operators were always very important and often hard to find!

The Popehn family came to Buck Hill in the late sixties and were an integral part of the business. Fran and Marie managed the rental department which was in the basement of the main chalet at that time. Their five children also worked at the area including Phil, Nannette, Grant, Greg, and Michelle. Another Buck Hill romance that led to marriage was that of Nannette Popehn and Dennis Rohrer.

Buck Hill also sparked many long lasting friendships. In July of 1967, Sookie Schlessinger joined the Buck Hill Ski Patrol. Sookie was born in Seoul, Korea and never had an opportunity to participate in any sports. She came to the United States in 1954 to attend Tufts University on a four-year scholarship. She came to Minnesota when her husband Paul was offered a job in Minneapolis at Campbell-Mithun. Paul was a skier and soon Sookie loved skiing as well. The spring of 1968, she was honored as the best Junior patroller of the year. She became an instructor in the ski school and eventually the secretary to manager Dick Lempke. Whenever she had a free moment she would get out on the slopes and practice her turns. Sookie had an amazing amount of good friends at Buck Hill including Mary Lempke, Bobbi Sipe*, and myself. Sookie

Buck Hill instructors in 1975: Ron Nebola, Horst Falger, Sookie Schlessinger, Roger Plath, Ursula Sailer, and Tom Sathre

and I even made a couple of trips to Lutsen and some other local ski areas. Sookie died suddenly of heart failure in December of 1993. She has been deeply missed. She was an iconic figure at Buck Hill.

Meanwhile, our highway struggles continued. On September 28, 1967, Chuck wrote a 7-page letter to David Durenberger, then Executive Secretary to Governor Le Vander in which he laid out in detail how the building of Highway 35W had so negatively affected Buck Hill. He enclosed the current financial statement in the letter as an exhibit. In Chuck's own words he began:

> For the past three years, Buck Hill has been confronted with a great many serious problems and expenses due to the construction and land acquisition of freeway 35W which bisects the property leased by Buck Hill. These problems which I will presently list will not contain details, as that is almost impossible. However, each one has been looked into by a qualified consultant and a report and appraisal has been submitted to Buck Hill.
>
> 1. Loss of a ski trail, which is irreplaceable.
>
> 2. Elimination of natural wind barrier by removing hills and trees.
>
> 3. By removing trees and hill, we now see instead – 4 lanes of traffic.
>
> 4. Security problems by extending the frontage road across the entire eastern border of the area.
>
> 5. Engineering problems: Mainly re-engineering of a new chair lift.
>
> 6. Flooding: No provisions were made for drainage by the State engineers on the project. Thus parking lots, the pump house area, garage, and maintenance shop have been under water numerous times.
>
> 7. Time: This not only includes employees of the company, but lawyers and appraisers as well. It is also alarming to know that the appraisers the state has hired have absolutely no experience in the ski business.
>
> 8. Loss of Business: It is impossible to know how many people have taken a look at this muddy mess and decided to go home or to another ski area.
>
> 9. Parking: The most pressing problem of all. We cannot operate a viable business if we do not have enough parking spaces for customers.

We have not been able to get our case to commissioners or into court in 3-1/2 years. The Highway department has done virtually nothing to solve our problems. As you might imagine, I could go on for hours where the Federal Government has put a great deal of money into the ski business, such as Lookout Mountain and Quadna Mountain and has not even received an interest payment. We are not asking for any federal or state handouts, but we would like a workable solution to our present urgent parking problem and the possibility of getting into court.

Negotiations continued and finally in 1968, the last payment from the Highway Department was made to Buck Hill bringing the total of compensation to $77,550. That was less than half the amount that we thought we deserved at the time. Of course, we were well aware that the exposure from the freeway has also contributed in some ways to the success of the business.

Buck Hill staff continued to come up with different ideas of how to attract more skiers to the hill. It was Stuart's idea to have a special program for ladies on a certain day of the week. He knew this had been successful at the course where he played golf. The idea was to highlight women's ski fashions and to attract them to the hill with a special package of lift, lesson and lunch. It proved to be very popular and was called Ladies Day.

Mrs. James Grogan (Sis) of Edina narrated the fashion show the first week, with fashions from Equinox Ski Shop being modeled during lunch hour. Judy Alm organized the models from the beginning. These included Sis and Judy as well as Marie Hudak, Carol Roth, Jackie Swendseen, Sherry Elmquist, and Jean Davis. Judy even skied in a bikini for the good of the cause. Barbara Flanagan, well known gossip columnist wrote in the *Minneapolis Star* "Howya gonna' keep 'em home in the kitchen after they've seen Buck Hill?"

Fashion Models, back: Toby Pohand, Gayle Rasmussen, Jo Vin Sant, Kitty Torntore, Judy Alm, and Charla Cartwright. Front: Jo Swendseen, Char Roe, Shirley Brenner, and Sis Grogan

There was very little bikini skiing in 1968. The bone chilling cold prompted the daily reports of the "wind chill factor," which is computed by measuring the temperature times the wind velocity. Wind chill factor became Minnesota's newest vehicle of hysteria. The media's constant preoccupation with "wind chill" was a considerable detriment to the ski business, causing skiers to stay home instead of heading out to ski (today it might be called fake news).

As Duane Netland described in a February 11, 1968 *Minneapolis Tribune* article, the focus on wind-chill was very misleading:

> Although, the temperature climbed to 6 above that day, yet the wind chill throughout the day measured around minus 27 degrees. Seth Kimball, manager of WCCO radio weather service said, "Wind chill is measured moreover on a body that is not moving." That prompted the inevitable retort from Kimball's good friend Buck Hills manager Stuart Campbell, "In other words," said Campbell, "it would be 27 below for a person standing naked on top of the hill." Campbell and several other operators were quick to point out that a skier is not only moving but heavily bundled in warm clothing. It is impossible to know what a damaging effect wind chill reporting has had on the ski business, but is something we have had to live with in the past and will continue to do in the future.

Although the winter of 1968 was extra chilly it did not stop Buck Hill employee Ned Gibowski from initiating and executing his famous flip on his 6'11" inch skis. Twenty-year old Ned made his first Stein Eriksen style flip at Buck Hill on January 15th before an audience of 300 skiers, and he continued to do so every Sunday throughout that winter. Ned became Buck Hill's rental shop manager in 1975. He eventually went to Sun Valley and became manager of one of their ski rental departments. We saw him there in the 80's.

We continued to try new ideas and make additional investments in the hill to improve the experience for our customers. In the fall of 1968, plastic snow, a 3-M product was tried at Buck Hill. One fall morning Chuck and I arrived early at the area and there were about 25 deer grazing on the "snow." Buck Hill was their home so they probably thought it was okay to have a little snack now and then. The deer all survived but the plastic snow experiment at that time did not.

The resident deer, enjoying a gourmet feast. Drawing by Emily Stone.

In 1968, we installed a 1,400 ft. Miner-Denver double chair lift with 58 chairs. It served Sleepy Hollow, an intermediate run, and Meadows, a recently finished beginners' slope. Night skiing was still a popular feature at Buck Hill with the area in full operation seven nights a week until 10:00 P.M. The illumination of the slopes (installed in the early 60's) was some of the best to be found in the Midwest. As the hill became re-contoured, runs named Nancy's Folly and Stone's Throw disappeared.

Around this time, the Stone family became involved in ski racing. We had brought the children to the ski area early in their lives and we taught them how to ski and ride a rope tow. They all became very good skiers and fortunately, inherited our love of the sport. They were outfitted in rubber ski boots and tiny skis which seemed to work very well. Cindy was the first of our three daughters to excel in ski racing. From the time she was eight years old she raced in the Buddy Werner League, which was a very strong junior racing program at the time for 12 year olds and under.

In the summer of 1969, Cindy attended the Red Lodge race camp in Red Lodge, Montana. The camp was owned by 3 ex-Austrian racers, Erich Sailer, Pepi Gramshammer, and Anderl Molterer. Cindy was aware that we were looking for a coach at Buck Hill and she heard Erich was looking for a job and thus put two and two together. Erich came to the area in the fall of 1969 as director of the Ski School, which included the racing team. The rest is history, which is covered later in the book. Another Red Lodge connection was that our daughter Polly first met her future husband Fridolf Hanson there when they were 13 years old.

By February 1969, Buck Hill was starting to receive national attention and was the focus of an article in *Skiing Magazine*. Stuart Campbell was interviewed and the emphasis was on snowmaking and night skiing. The article mentioned Buck Hill's ski school, its children's programs, and even its Adult Learn to Ski program. It spoke of its existing facilities and the explosive growth Buck Hill was experiencing due to its reinvestment and attention to upgrading the business.

In 1969, Chuck and I went on a business ski trip

70's Tucker Sno-Cat and old T-Bar, soon to be replaced with a chair lift.

(the most fun kind) to the east and visited many different ski areas with the purpose of seeing first hand what was new and working well. Some of the areas were Glen Ellyn, Stowe, Madonna Mountain, Cannon Mountain, Waterville Valley, and Loon Mountain. We saw Jean Claude Killy and other high profile international skiing stars at a World Cup race at Waterville Valley. The most fun and interesting part of the trip for Chuck was talking with the owners and employees. At Stowe, we met Sepp Ruschp, an Austrian born skier who was president and general manager of the Mount Mansfield Company and who also helped develop recreational and competitive skiing throughout the United States. He took Chuck to check out the maintenance shop which was one of the highlights of the trip for him. The shop manager told him they have 9 Tuckers, 3 Sprites and several John Deere tractors and he thought the Tucker was the easiest to maintain and keep running (I saw a hint of envy in Chuck's eyes at this point). Most of the areas were charging $10.00 per day for skiing. We learned a great deal and felt that many of the areas in the East were doing a good job in all respects, except snow grooming. However, we did get some good ideas to take back to Powder Ridge and Buck Hill.

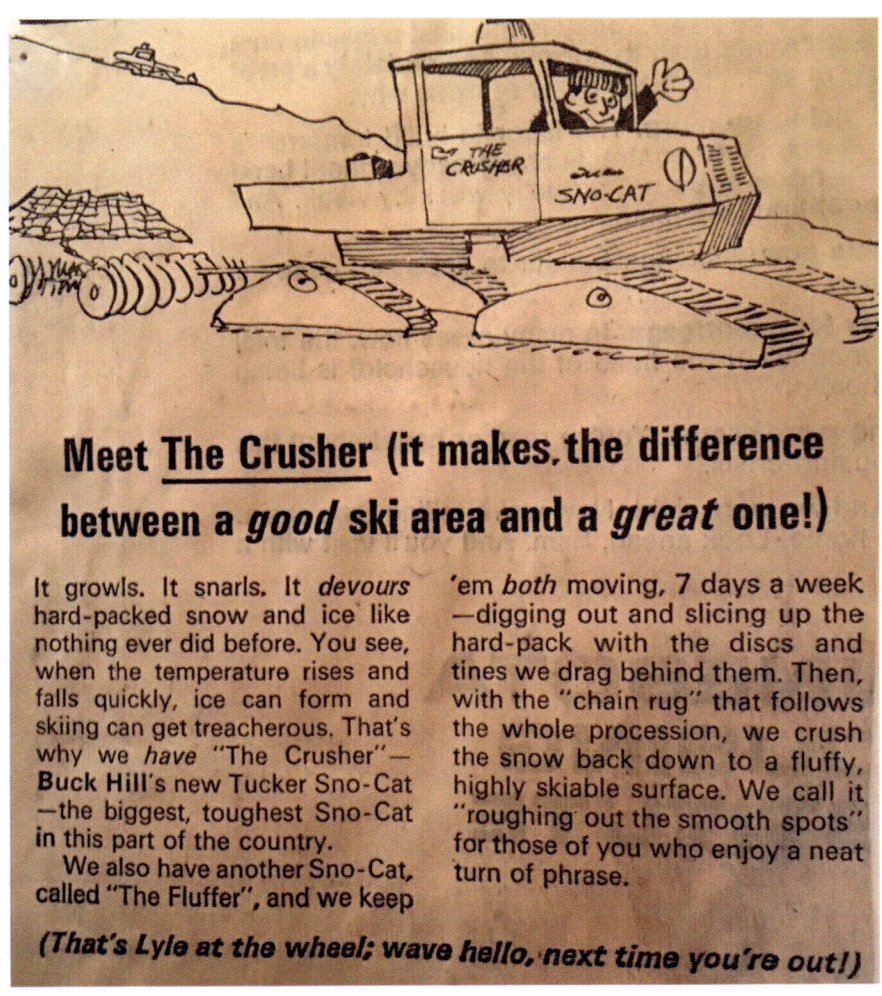

Meet The Crusher (it makes the difference between a *good* ski area and a *great* one!)

It growls. It snarls. It *devours* hard-packed snow and ice like nothing ever did before. You see, when the temperature rises and falls quickly, ice can form and skiing can get treacherous. That's why we *have* "The Crusher"— **Buck Hill**'s new Tucker Sno-Cat —the biggest, toughest Sno-Cat in this part of the country.

We also have another Sno-Cat, called "The Fluffer", and we keep 'em *both* moving, 7 days a week —digging out and slicing up the hard-pack with the discs and tines we drag behind them. Then, with the "chain rug" that follows the whole procession, we crush the snow back down to a fluffy, highly skiable surface. We call it "roughing out the smooth spots" for those of you who enjoy a neat turn of phrase.

(That's Lyle at the wheel; wave hello, next time you're out!)

The Buck Hill guys invented The Crusher.
Artwork by Tony Sellwood.

THE SEVENTIES

Tucker Sno-Cat, Powder Ridge, Hutch Chalet, Gawn Inc, New Chairlifts for Both Areas, Energy Crisis, McDonalds Cup, Graduated Length Method, Dick Lempke, Gabe Cyr, Quad Chairlift, New Restaurant/Bar, SkyRide

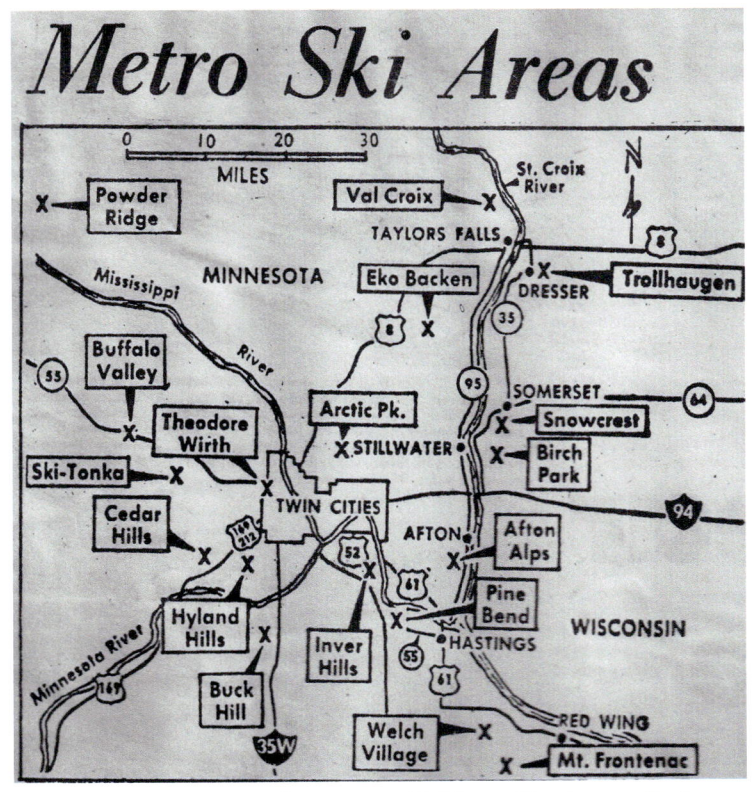

In November 1970, there were 19 Metro Ski Areas. Today, only eight of them remain in business.

The seventies began with a bang as the snow and temperatures cooperated and the winter season of 1969-1970 proved to be a record one. We did some fine tuning of the various programs at Buck Hill and with new funding in place we were able to purchase a 900 series Tucker Sno-Cat with a pulling capacity of 6,000 pounds. This made it possible to groom the entire area in three hours.

Chris Klass, Brooks Sellwood, Andrew Howell, Larry Howell, Tim Sellwood, Rick Howell, Chuck Stone III

At Powder Ridge, some cross country ski trails had been added. Another new attraction was "Tucker Jumping." Gary Hansen, ski school director, and other instructors, patrolmen, and experts would leap 75 feet into the air on their skis over the Sno-Cat. The Tucker was also used to groom the slopes when it was not used for fun.

Gary Hansen "Tucker Jumping." It was also used for grooming at Powder Ridge.

Powder Ridge also started a very popular "Bring Your Own Steak Night" on Thursday nights with the ski area supplying free hors d'oeuvres, salad, bread, coffee, and cooking the meat in its huge fireplace. According to New Hampshire consultant Sel Hannah, Powder Ridge had the best kiddie slope in the nation. Powder Ridge proved it had a soft heart by hosting the Consolation Bowl for junior skiers who didn't make the cut for the regional races.

Steve Bauer contributed to this history with some treasured memories of his years working at Buck Hill. He served as chalet manager between the mid sixties and the mid seventies. Those years were only interrupted by his two years of service in Vietnam. Steve wrote:

Dennis Rohrer was the outside hill manager who oversaw all the construction projects and crews. The summer of 1971 saw major building for a new ski school, ski area office, and the Hutch Chalet for small groups and parties. Buck Hill always strived to be the Midwest leader in ski area innovation. We made snowmaking upgrades which included home made snow guns that were mounted on poles and towers throughout the area. We built the first version of today's snow tiller, know as The Crusher, which is now used world wide at every ski resort in their snow grooming operations. Buck Hill also expanded into a year round business, installing everything from a mountain coaster, artificial snow, and Frisbee golf, to utilize the facilities and keep employees for the entire year.

Buck Hill was on the cutting edge with regards to the technology it used to make the area more efficient and profitable. As the Tucker Sno Cat went from steel rollers to rubber tracks, it became apparent that the maintenance would be greatly reduced, prompting Stuart and Chuck to think the Sno Cat would be a good franchise opportunity for Buck Hill. GAWN, Inc. was formed as a wholly owned subsidiary of Buck Hill, Inc. on August 15, 1971 to function as a distributor of ski area management equipment. The Crusher, a grooming implement, was one of the first products of GAWN.

Other significant long time employees were Fred Peterson, Doug Buerke, Gary McNevin and Lynn Throne. Fred has some memories of his own:

I started at Buck Hill in the spring of 1959 to help cut down some trees. In the spring of 1966, I graduated from Dunwoody College. Wages earned at Buck Hill paid for that tuition. I did ski lift maintenance and supervised the ski lift operation until 1975. During this time another employee Steve Havig showed me an article on how to build a ski bike in the February 1966 issue of *Popular Mechanics Magazine*. Steve built one and I tried it out and was hooked. Taking up ski bobbing now called snow biking, in the spring of 1966 has created a passion that has taken me to 29 countries and 132 ski areas around the world. Buck Hill allowed me to hone my skills acquired at Dunwoody, which led to a successful 35-year career owning a carnival games operation. I really enjoyed working at Buck Hill as I think many of us did.

At the time, two chair lifts were manufactured by Buck Hill personnel (one for Powder Ridge, and one for Buck Hill) and put under the GAWN, Inc. name. In 1973, Buck Hill became the Midwestern distributor for Tucker Sno-Cats which were manufactured in Medford, Oregon. Steve Bauer became involved with the management and did an excellent job. Sales grew each year and by 1973 they had increased to $319,000. The company's future seemed to be extremely bright as Tucker was the Cadillac of the snow vehicle field and, as the product got more exposure, continued sales growth was expected. We also continued to get favorable exposure from the local press.

Bob Goligoski wrote an article about Powder Ridge in the *Minneapolis*

Tribune December 1, 1972 titled **Farm, Ski Areas Merge at Kimball**:

After our recent jaunt to the slopes, we were pleasantly surprised by the quality and amount of the man-made snow. Gone was the infamous "Minnesota hardpack" replaced by a layer of light fluff. Swishing through the woods, one is more likely to hear the neighing and crooning of nearby horses and cows instead of a cheerful yodel from one of the Austrian Instructors.

But one is quickly immersed in ski scene atmosphere once more as the thick Austrian accent of Maria Neubauer drifts over the snow, announcing the start of lessons or the race results from the weekly children's competition. Maria's husband Geog Neubauer is the ski school director. His staff of 20 full and part time instructors offered the graduated length method (start on short skis and work up to long ones) and other techniques.

Ben Kern wrote an article in the *Minneapolis Tribune* December 15, 1972, about how Powder Ridge and Buck Hill both had a Midwest feel:

Distinguishing characteristics are Powder Ridge's country flavor and unabashed Upper Midwestern look. It shares the latter with Buck Hill. You can't stand on either Buck Hill or Powder Ridge and imagine you are anywhere else. Buck Hill overlooks the Minneapolis skyline and Powder Ridge overlooks miles of cornfields.

Both articles mentioned the amenities at the two ski areas. There was a lot of interest in the growing sport of alpine skiing and the newspapers were diligent in covering that interest and all of the ski areas were very grateful.

In the summer of 1972, significant capital improvements were made in areas which were hard for the skier to appreciate. A great deal of money was spent on such items as electrical compressors, pumps, new roofs and so on. These expenditures, though needed, were not as noticed by skiing guests as some of our previous

Sunny day at Buck Hill in 1973.

capital improvements had been. Income tended to level off and servicing the debt became more expensive. Taxes increased and we found ourselves in somewhat of an unfavorable position. At the same time, many new competitive ski areas were opened which were primarily aimed at Buck Hill's market. Our assets began to deteriorate and refurbishment was needed to remain competitive. This situation proved to be a difficult obstacle for us, but not unique, as most businesses face similar issues from time to time.

There was a move in 1972 by three board members to buy the Stone family stock in Buck Hill and I thank our lucky stars it did not happen. It was a very traumatic time (which spanned a few years), for Chuck and all of our family. When the buy-out agreement stipulated that he had to stay out of the ski business, Chuck said, "The deal is off," and he returned as Chairman of the Board and back to all of his other previous commitments.

In 1973, the Energy Crisis was in full swing and it lingered throughout the 70's. OPEC raised the price of oil dramatically from $2.00 a barrel to more than $12.00 a barrel. Americans waited in line for gas and paid higher prices. This increase affected the ski industry in many ways. The price of all utilities rose and that added to the ski areas' operating expenses. We thought this might possibly be a benefit to areas that were closer to the cities because of the shorter driving time, but of course that was impossible to know.

Chuck was always interested in the possibility of buying other areas. At this time, it was Grand Targhee in Idaho and Pine Bend in St. Paul. Extensive research was done on both areas but it was not to be.

In 1973, the World Pro Ski Tour came to Buck Hill. This organization was founded by Bob Beattie back in 1969, who had previously been the U.S. Ski Team head coach from 1961-1969. He was aware of the deep commitment Buck Hill had to racing and that was one of the reasons he approached us to hold a pro race. The race was held in conjunction with the St. Paul Winter Carnival. It was sponsored by McDonald's and Benson & Hedges and was called the McDonald's Cup Pro Ski Classic. This was the first head to head pro race in Minnesota and it proved to be an exciting event. The Benson & Hedges Grand Prix year book

Ready for the McDonald's Cup to start

described the race at Buck Hill:

> Long, steep courses may be tough but short, flat ones are murderous. That was the feeling at the $20,000 McDonalds's Cup at Buck Hill, Minnesota. The sixth stop on the Benson & Hedges Tour was a changeup – the slow ball after three fast balls that makes the batter swing and miss and look like a fool. Only Trappeur's Jean Claude Killy, who won the giant slalom, and K'2s Spider Sabich, who took the slalom were able to adjust, but even they did not adjust completely. Killy was skiing competitively for the first time since he won all three Alpine skiing gold medals in the 1968 Olympics in Grenoble, France. Killy said that it was a very easy course, which made it more difficult to win. He believed that one could ski it well, but if you made a mistake and lose your lead you could not regain it.

Walter Bush recalled on the day the race took place Jean Claude Killy told him, that when he drove by Buck Hill, he couldn't imagine a professional ski race being held in "the flat lands." To his amazement, the race was very successful and was a springboard to Sunday's race.

Jessica Stone getting some racing tips from Spider Sabich.

Suzy Chafee, Polly Stone, and Ronald McDonald

In January of 1974, Jean Claude Killy was in town again to promote his new book, **Comeback**. In the book he mentioned Buck Hill since the 1973 McDonald's Cup race at Buck Hill was the very first professional race held there and was where Killy's professional comeback began the previous year.

The second McDonald's Pro Ski Classic Cup races were held at Buck Hill January 18-20th 1974, during Killy's book

Mary Lempke, Stuart Campbell, Rita Dalrymple, and J.C. Killy watching the race.

tour visit, but he could not race because of an ulcer. He commented, "I wish I were out there with the others. Buck Hill, you see, is a flat hill, not steep, where I ski the best. So the "skater" skiers who can push off at each gate and actually accelerate while they are going through do better. In pro-racing, two skiers race simultaneously on side by side courses, switching for a second run, with the lowest combined time winning the heat. Buck Hill will surprise a lot of racers." Killy muttered, "Fantistique!" the first time he saw the 313-foot-high Minnesota hill. "If you don't concentrate every second you can lose 3 feet to your opponent and never get it back."

J.C. Killy and many of his admirers.

In the '74 McDonald's Cup, Austrian, Hugo Nindl, a 30-year-old hotel owner, won the giant slalom, and barely beat fellow Austrian Harald Staufer by .555 of a second, winning the $4,000 first place. The following day, Nindl beat Spider Sabich to win the Slalom event.

As Chuck was always open to another ski race, he came up with the idea of having Buck Hill host a Region I "Homecoming" for racing alumni that would be home from college at Christmas time. It would also allow the local regional competitors to have a "scored" race before the national points list update on January 1st. He talked with USSA and got the race on the calendar and named it the Buck Hill Christmas Race. The top seed traditionally included U.S. Ski Team members, collegiate team members, as well as top local and occasionally foreign competitors as well. In 1981, local elite competitor Ara Burwell was tragically killed in an airplane accident and the race was re-named the "Ara Burwell Memorial." The race continues today as the marquis national point race in the region and the entire Central Division. It was renamed in 1995 in honor of Chuck and now called the "Chuck Stone Memorial Race."

Amateur racing was also popular at the hill. In 1976, Buck Hill was the only ski area in Minnesota with a NASTAR franchise. Individual racers compete against the pacesetters at the area who, at that time were Jim Holst and Doug Nordmeyer*, both accomplished racers from the Buck Hill Team. These two raced against top professional skiers. The pacesetter's handicap is the time percentage the NASTAR racer is behind these pros.

In 1975, our racing team's assistant coach, Andrzej Derezinski, introduced Eva and Marian Polakiewicz* to the Buck Hill ski area and it became their winter home. Andrzej was a member of Polish Alpine Olympic Team (Insbruck) 1964. Andrzej and Marian were NASTAR pacesetters at Buck Hill. Before he came to the USA, Marian worked with the Polish National Alpine Ski Team as assistant coach for 7 years. He traveled to World Cup races. Marian worked as the racing team's equipment manager for Buck Hill for decades. Eva remembers:

Eva and Marian Polakiewicz qualified four times for the NASTAR finals.

We have always appreciated Buck Hill's race friendly operation and we have participated in NASTAR and Ski Challenge races. In the old days you had to be in the top ten of your age group in the nation to qualify for NASTAR finals. We were invited four times and we represented Buck Hill. In particular I remember GS training with Chuck Stone. The course was set by Brad Kastner. I asked Chuck if I could ski the course. "Yes," he answered, "...after you Eva." Chuck was really a gentleman. This was one of my best memories.

As Buck Hill continued to grow, I kept very busy with a different ski related venture. In the summer of 1974, I started a company called EWE FIRST. My partner Colleen Walter and I designed wool hats and sweaters and they were knit by women in their homes on knitting machines, a true cottage industry. Of course our first customer was Buck Hill. We soon branched out and sold hats to many of the ski shops in the Twin Cities and an order of 10 dozen or more was not uncommon.

We also did special orders for clubs and teams. Cindy Stone was living in Vail at the time, and she had many accounts in Vail and Aspen, as well as special orders such as World Cup hats, which originated with our company. We were

quite successful and had a lot of fun with it. It was especially satisfying to see our hats on skiers in national ski magazines. In fact, Chuck and I saw three Ewe First hats on skiers while we were standing in a lift line in Switzerland and gazing at the Eiger. This was before helmets became so popular. Although successful, I had too many other commitments so I sold the business in 1991.

Special order of EWE FIRST knit hats.

During this same time, my friend, Carolyn Cole Schwantes, had introduced me to the Hammer School which provided a home for people with developmental disabilities. In the seventies, we initiated a skiing program and took about ten residents to Hyland Hills for a few hours of downhill skiing every week. My special buddy was Kevin. We had a lot of fun, but the program ended when the residents became enrolled in the public schools.

Clock tower at Mont Le Buc

Ned Gibowski at the ski show in the convention center.

Chuck had such magnificent dreams for Buck Hill. Many that he visualized did not come true, but they were often replaced with ones that did. He always believed Buck Hill would be an ideal place for a resort hotel and maybe some day it will be. Meanwhile, one of his wishes included a clock tower which was built in the fall of 1976. Of course, if you look at the hill behind it, you will know at a glance that you are not in Vail. However, you will now be able to see the correct time from either the Milk Run or the highway; but don't look too long.

The first printing of the *Buck Hill Express*, a weekly in-house newspaper, came out on November 6, 1975 and stated that: "According to the new rental shop manager, Ned Gibowski, the rental shop will have 400 sets of new equipment, which includes Hart short skis, Manari boots and Spademan bindings. Spademans are considered to be one of the safest and quickest step-in bindings on the market. Rentals are used by all skiers in the Graduated Length Method (GLM) ski school program and most of the other beginner lesson programs."

In 1975, Chuck laid out his plans for the future of the company in a twenty-page document, titled **A Planning Program for Buck Hill, Inc**. by Chuck Stone. The plan stated that:

Buck Hill, Inc.'s goals should be: (1) to provide adequate financing for the companies – Buck Hill, Powder Ridge, and Gawn. (2) to develop each of its company's facilities, capacities, and business to the fullest extent for profit. (3) to investigate and seek new recreational opportunities near metropolitan areas where our expertise would be valuable, (4) to investigate the possibilities of becoming involved in a mountain type complex.

Buck Hill was hopeful that the '75-'76 season would shape up to be a more normal season weather wise than the previous one. January of '75 was probably one of the best on record in terms of ticket sales. However, February of that year proved to be one of the worst! The warm weather in February virtually ended the season by mid month but Buck Hill still managed to serve 100,000 skiers, an indication of continuing growth in traffic for close-in hills. In November, the Hutch Chalet was remodeled, complete with an enclosed, heated sun deck and a large fireplace. It was for adults only on weekends and private parties during the week.

In April of 1976, Stuart Campbell resigned as president and general manager of the ski area. He bought GAWN, Inc. from Buck Hill and renamed it Track, Inc. Although Stuart left Buck Hill, his reputation in the ski industry continued to grow. Steve Bauer also left at this time to work with Stuart at Track, Inc. The business turned out to be a very successful enterprise and the company expanded at a rapid pace. Track, Inc. grew to become the largest distributor of Tucker Sno Cats in North America.

Kitchen manager, Jo Henning, 1976

In 1976, Dick Lempke became the new general manger at Buck Hill. He started at the ski area when he was 13 picking up rocks in the summer for a season pass. He went on to ticket-taking, flipping burgers, and just about everything else. He studied accounting at the University of Minnesota and did some bookkeeping too. After 16 years, he became general manager with a lot of responsibility. In addition to Dick Lempke, Dick Caswell was in charge of public relations, Erich and Ursula Sailer headed the ski school and race team, Doug Burke was the outside manager, Jim Shea served as the lift manager, and Jo Hanning was the kitchen manager. Ken Goewey, who had been at Powder Ridge as chalet manager, came to Buck Hill about this time and continued in that capacity.

Gary Ladd,* the new Rossignol rep, came to Buck Hill in the fall of 1976 after seeing Buck Hill in

Gary Ladd, our invaluable Rossignol Representative.

the movie **Spyder and the Frenchman** by Dick Barrymore. We did not know how lucky we were at the time. Gary provided good advice and lots of skis for many of the racers on the Buck Hill team, and was still doing so in 2015.

In October of 1977, Chuck wrote a letter to the shareholders reporting that most of the summer had been spent repairing and maintaining both ski areas and felt they were in very good shape for the coming season. Major improvements were made at Powder Ridge that summer. These included the addition of 30 vertical feet to the top of Gun-Powder and the installation of a new Riblet double chair lift. The lighting and snow-making were also expanded. At Buck Hill, a new rope tow was installed on the Freeway run and the quartz lights in the parking lot were replaced with metal halide lights. In addition, a new 1600 Tucker Sno-Cat

Installing underground snowmaking pipe on the J-Bar Hill.

was acquired which greatly improved our grooming capacity. Another great addition in 1977 was that Gabe Cyr joined the staff at Buck Hill as director of adult racing. We also introduced the Buck Hill Ski Team Swap that year and it has been a very successful fund raiser for the team ever since. Chuck continued to have discussions with Red Lodge Ski Area about the possibility of a sale or a merger but sadly it did not materialize.

In March of 1978, Gregg Wong of the *St. Paul Pioneer Press* interviewed Gabe Cyr about spring skiing. "At our ski association meetings we talked about how we might get skiers out late in the season," said Mrs. Cyr. Gabe and her late husband Oscar were the owners of the old Pine Bend Ski Area for 20 years from 1952-1972 before the area closed after a dispute with the nearby refineries. And if there is anyone who knows the ski business, it's Gabe Cyr.

Gabe had become bored with retirement and realized how much she missed the ski business. So when Chuck came along and asked her to come and work at Buck Hill she jumped at the chance, and it was a wonderful year for her and the area. She hadn't skied since 1965, but the business was in her blood. Gabe thought the people at Buck Hill were the greatest to work with. She believed that they cared about each other and the skiers.

According to Gabe:

That's why Chuck Stone agonizes every time he sees a ski lift stop. It is important to him that the skier has a good time. There will be a lot of good things going on here next year, including a new quad chair lift. But I might add, there is still plenty of skiing left this season – so why not give your favorite area another fling or two?

Paul Swanson* joined the Buck Hill crew in the summer of 1978 to help out on the construction of the new quad chairlift and chalet. By opening day in November, Paul had become inside manager, responsible for ticketing, food service oversight, and building maintenance. He also helped out with snowmaking and relieving the chairlift operators. Paul later moved on to work with Stuart Campbell at Track Inc.

There were many improvements for the 1978-1979 season. Thirty feet of vertical rise was added to the top of the hill. A state of the art quad chairlift replaced the old temperamental T-Bar that had served the skiers since 1961. The new face of Buck Hill featured the runs Crossroads and Milk Run. A two level restaurant-bar designed by architects Kilstoffe and Vasejpke was ready for the upcoming winter season. A redesigned entrance from Buck Hill Road, additional parking, and a larger drop-off area completed the changes. These were significant additions that we were very excited about. The 78-79 winter season turned out to be the second best in the area's history as the skiing public was thrilled with the these improvements.

In a newspaper called *Ski Week*, the September 1979 issue Chuck commented on the difference in skiing at Buck Hill in 1954 when we first opened with the current skiing. "Skiers were quite a bit different in those days, said Stone. The runs were quite narrow down thru the trees and there were a few bare spots. There wasn't any grooming equipment either. Today skiers like a lot of room to move around in and are much more demanding than in the 50's. The whole sport has changed dramatically. There were no safety bindings and I remember skiing on 220cm skis; that's about 7'5"."

In the late 70's, free-style competitor Tom Kelly, a member of the Buck Hill Freestyle Team, had some significant results. He placed second in the junior division ballet competition of the United States Skiing Association National Freestyle Championships at Jackson, Wyoming. Tom was a junior at Apple Valley High School at the time. Tom won the nationals the following year. The team was aptly coached by Bob Turgeon. Tom earned his season pass by doing odd jobs around the hill and there was always an abundance of those.

Chuck wrote a brief history of the hill and from this I quote, "Growth continued unabated until 1978 when demand tended to level off. During the same period, approximately 400 ski areas in the United States had gone out of business. However, those areas that remained showed real growth capacity in terms of lifts and trails."

Once again in the summer of 1979, we made a very dedicated effort to establish a summer business. If successful, it could have made such a difference in revenue and cash flow for a ski area that is constantly in need of capital improvements. We held a Media Day on June 1 with the opening of a new restaurant called the Sports Bucket and summer sports center. A Mountain coaster had also been installed on the hill. The Buck Hill press release said:

> Come one, come all, downhill riders, volleyball players, Frisbee golfers, horseshoe pitchers, croquet players, basket shooters, eaters, light-wine and beer drinkers, maybe a lollygagger or two – action awaits you. (Chuck was about 30 years ahead of his time with Frisbee golf). The mountain coaster is a 1,680-foot monorail down Milk Run, one of Buck's most advanced ski runs. The coaster carrying a $100,000 price tag, has five sharp banked curves and two roller coaster type dips over its length. Speeds of up to 30 miles an hour can be reached, according to one of the coasters operators.

Governor Al Quie, Mayor Paul Scheunemann, State Representative Chuck Halberg, and Chamber of Commerce President Robert Christensen were present for the dedication ceremony.

We put a lot of time, money and enthusiasm into making this summer venture a success but sadly it was not. We closed the operation the end of the summer in 1980, but Chuck did not give up, he had more ideas.

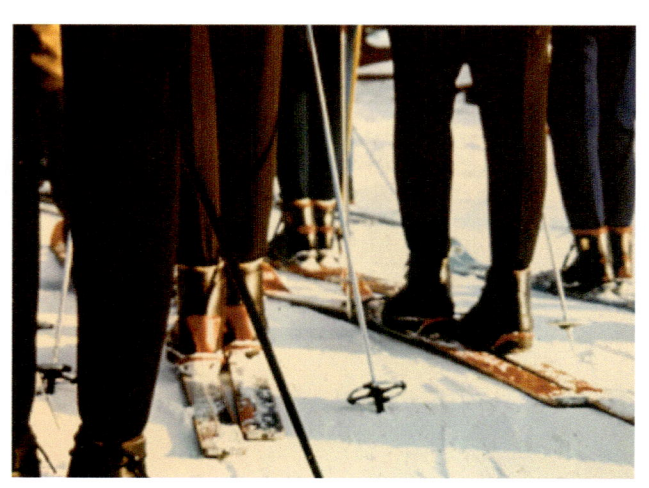

Governor Al Quie attending the Grand Opening of the Mountain Coaster.

Ski ya later, back to the winter season!

THE EIGHTIES

Lenny Lightfingers, Lempke Returns, Vandermint Dutch Coffee Cup, Telemarketing, Grace Whittier, Guaranteed Learn to Ski, Jerry Wahlin, Ski Challenge, Government Intrusion, Snowboarding

Artist Marlee Brown painted this beautiful picture of sunny Buck Hill.

The eighties began with a few challenges as Dick Lempke resigned as general manager to take a position at Welch Village. After an extensive search we hired a new manager from the East. To protect his identity, I will call him "Lenny Lightfingers" as he admitted to "borrowing" $4,000.00 from the company. I was back doing the books that summer and came across a Buck Hill check made out to a car company, so once again we were without a general manager and Lenny was without a new car and a job.

I remember one sultry August day, I was up in the office doing some bookkeeping, when all of a sudden the sky turned an ominous color, the wind picked up and then the sirens went off. I knew Don McClure was down in the maintenance shed, but I wasn't sure that he would save me, so I went down to the ladies' room in the basement. I wondered if my life was going to end in the Buck Hill bathroom after all these years, but it turned out there wasn't even a tornado.

The ski season of 1980-1981 was not a good one for the whole country mainly due to the very warm weather. Nationwide business was down 27%, while Buck Hill and Powder Ridge were down 24%. The next season was just as challenging. In fact, the first 3 years of the 80's were also difficult. However, we were able to install 11,000 feet of 6-inch pipe at both areas for more efficient snow-making and Dick Lempke returned as general manager. J. R. Stevens took over the role of controller in the early 80's. Ed Carducci was food and beverage manager at this time. We continued to look for ways to grow revenue. At a board meeting that year, we decided to apply for a liquor license for the bar and restaurant on our land that was north of the Whittier property.

Snowmaking, 1981. Marty Sutter with homemade snow gun.

Johnson, West and Company continued to be our accounting firm. At this point in time, Dan St. Martin was the man in charge of our account. He and his assistant came out to do the audit at the end of the summer in our tiny non-air conditioned office. There was a blizzard of flies attacking Dan and he accused Dick of training them to bug him so they would get the audit done sooner. Dick wanted his office back.

Excitement reigned as The Vandermint Dutch Coffee Cup came to Buck Hill in January of 1982. The women professional racers came early to spend a day with local women skiers of all levels of expertise. The professionals were Vicki Fleckenstein, Susie Patterson, Jamie Kurlander, and Mary Seaton of the United

States, Jocelyne Perillat of France, Lise-Marie Morerod of Switzerland, and Toril Forland of Norway. The clinic, also sponsored by Ski Hut, was for all levels of woman skiers and was in conjunction with the women's ski races that took place January 28-30. The package included a full day's activity, a continental breakfast and a clinic with the pro racers and Buck Hill instructors. There was a luncheon with guest speakers, an afternoon clinic, an evaluation session and ending with a wine and cheese party. This race was one of nine stops on the 1981-1982 circuit with a total purse of $100,000. The women raced in side by side courses of slalom and giant slalom. It turned out to be a very successful event with Vicki Fleckenstein finishing first and Jamie Kurlander in second place.

Vicki Fleckenstein was the overall winner of the Vandermint Cup.

Our nephew, Bruce Freeman[*] is one of the most dedicated Buck Hill fans that I know. From a very early age he was very interested in the ski business and I imagine that was because he loved to ski so much. He had opinions and ideas galore and he has been a faithful skier in all kinds of conditions. Bruce and Chuck spent many hours discussing current situations and future plans for the area. Bruce was also a very competent carpenter and had his skills put to use at Buck Hill on many occasions. He built decks, lift houses, worked on the starting ramp, and lent his hand to some of the haunts at Frightmares.

On January 31, 1982, Ben Kern of the *Minneapolis Tribune* wrote a lengthy article about Bruce, then director of the Buck Hill-Rossignol Telemark Center, and organizer of the Midwest Telemark Series of races. He also wrote about his own lesson at Buck Hill with Bruce. In the article Bruce was quoted as saying "I became so fascinated with the Telemark turn that I vowed to learn it.... Now I want to give you that same opportunity to experience all that excitement and joy." Kern took him up on that and reported, "I made some progress, but I had one codger-like problem. I had done my early telemarking in moderate temperatures on comfortably wide skis. Trying to repeat what I remembered, in a subzero wind, on skinny skis, I got off to a

Bruce Freeman made Telemarking look easy.

very wobbly start."

Ben was a good sport to attempt the Telemark on a really frigid day! He was a great fan of Buck Hill and wrote many favorable articles about us. In fact, this is an appropriate time to thank all of the journalists that were loyal fans of Buck Hill and all the other local ski areas as well. They did an excellent job of promoting the sport, and many actually participated as well.

The Buck Hill board of directors met at the Decathalon Club on May 18, 1983. Chuck reported that "it had not been a good year in the ski business. The attendance was down 18% from the 1981-1982 season and many smaller areas had gone out of business. Utility expenses were up and another added expense this year is the assessment for the storm sewer in Burnsville." The board complimented Dick Lempke and Ron Greely on their jobs in controlling labor and other expenses during the season. Chuck's report specified: "there will only be minor improvements made at the area, mostly in the Adult Racing Program Department. These will include a racing office above the patrol room to house new computers and provide more room for the race officials. There will be two new display boards visible to skiers, which print out the time and computerized NASTAR handicaps for both courses. It will be the finest racing set up in the area, in keeping with our motto of "your number 1 at Buck Hill." Chuck continued to work on the concept of "Wellness" for a conference center at the hill.

1984 began sadly for us as Grace Whittier, who was born on October 20 1895 died on January 25th. Chuck and I considered Grace a very good friend. We had a very good personal and business relationship and met with her at least twice a year, often in Northfield. I am quoting a paragraph from the program at her memorial service at United Methodist Church in Northfield:

Miss Whittier was a descendant of some of the oldest Rice County residents, her Drake grandparents having arrived in the early 1850's. She was a direct descendant of Sir Francis Drake, and her great-grandmother was Martha Clark Drake, a sister of the Clark of the Lewis and Clark Expedition. On her father's side, she shared common ancestry with John Greenleaf Whittier the famous poet. She was a graduate of Carleton College and earned an MA degree from the University of Southern California. She held a variety of interesting positions in the fields of personnel and teaching. She was very involved in the community of Northfield and was honored several times."

In 2001, we named the banquet room in the new Buckstone Lodge the Whittier Room in memory of Grace.

Upon her death, the land we leased for Buck Hill was left to St. Olaf College. It was a mystery to us as to why Grace would leave her Buck Hill property to St. Olaf College when both she and her father were graduates of Carleton College.

In **The Slope Man Cometh** article about Chuck and Buck Hill in the *Minnetonka Magazine* by Ann Anderson, Ann captured Chuck's philosophy of how to run a successful ski area: "Despite adversities, Stone continues to be optimistic and urges people to forget about wind chill temperatures, to ski all conditions and above all to have fun." Chuck added "Buck Hill has a larger ratio of good skiers than any place I have been. Most important, I know that our skiers experience results whether free skiing or racing, and that's gratifying to me."

Buck Hill was a very popular venue for NASTAR. We held NASTAR races at the hill every Friday evening and Sunday afternoon. This NASTAR press release from Aspen, Colorado in 1983 best describes the program:

NASTAR is the world's largest recreational ski racing program, with events conducted on a regular basis throughout the winter at 120 ski resorts in the United States. In NASTAR, recreational skiers of all ages and abilities race against a National Standard which is established each fall, in order to compare themselves with other NASTAR skiers and with a national standard.

In the 1968-69 season there were 8 ski areas involved with 2,297 entrants. By the winter of 1981-82 there were 121 ski areas with 223,738 participants. Buck Hill was consistently one of the top areas to send the most number of racers to the finals which were usually held in the west. Adult racing clinics were held on Friday nights and Sundays. In the eighties these clinics were coached by Kevin Arms, Dave Thorson, and Tim Buckley.

NASTAR Championship Steamboat Springs, 1984. 1st Place - No. 71 Tom Temple, 2nd Place - No. 68 Bob Tengdin, 3rd Place - No. 72 Erik Tolleffson, 4th Place - No. 67 Charles McCarthy

In March of 1985, Buck Hill's NASTAR racer Shelly Adams and her father Rick made history as the first father-daughter combination to make the NASTAR finals which were in Sun Valley, Idaho that year. Nineteen year old Shelly captured the 18-29 age group while her father was eighth in the 40-49 age group. Buck Hill sent Jim Holst along as their private coach and he told Shelly to growl as she went through the gates. It must have worked.

In 1984, *The Minneapolis Star Tribune* sponsored a local challenge to the Twin City ski areas. It was called "Guaranteed Learn to Ski." Chuck embraced the concept and challenge. Buck Hill received a National Ski Area Association award of $1500.00 for the best program to interest entry level skiiers into the sport. An article in the *St. Paul Dispatch*, by David Smith, January 1984, was one of the most informative articles I have seen on this subject and it was sure to make beginners much more confident about their ability to learn to ski. David wrote:

CLASSES HELPING DOWNHILL SKIERS GLIDE TO NEW GOALS: The major areas in and around the Twin Cities offer a variety of instruction to suit just about any skier's needs. There are day and evening classes in everything from ballet skiing to slalom racing. There are kinder schools for children as young as three. For people who thought they could never learn to ski, there are several "guaranteed-learn-to ski" programs that will have you out carving arcs in the snowpack within a few days – or you get your money back.

Jerry Wahlin, New General Manager at Powder Ridge.

In the summer of 1984, Jerry Wahlin became the general manager of Powder Ridge. Ron Greely had resigned and taken a position at Giants Ridge Ski Area. Jerry had previously been Mountain Manager at Trollhaugen Ski Area in Dresser, Wisconsin. Jerry and his wife Jane moved to the Kimball area and have never left. Together they raised 3 children, Andrea, Samantha, and Casey, who believe Powder Ridge is the center of the skiing world.

Also in 1984, Chris Heid came to work at Buck Hill and his first job was in the kitchen and George Kukucha was the manager at that time. It was a family affair as Chris's brother and three sisters were also employed at the area. Chris moved from kitchen to cash room, and in 1993 he found he was outside as a lift supervisor. That was a big job which required many skills; just keeping the schedules for every operator was challenging in itself. Chris also did some carpentry with Geno as there were always new projects and things in need of repair. At a small ski area, hard-working men with many skills like Chris

Chris Heid putting the ski area to sleep after a long winter.

were very valuable employees.

An important development in 1984 was the beginning of the SKI CHALLENGE. It was founded by Patricia Lecy and De Bourdaghs and the purpose of it was to provide an opportunity for adults to race for fun! There were 35 participants that first year and by 2015 there were 1,200 racers ages four to some in their eighties. The Challenge is made up of leagues with ten racers in each league. Since 1997 it has been owned by Dave and Barb Evenson and affiliated with Padraig's Place.

The Twin Cities Ski Challenge presented plaques to its eight sponsors at the December Open Houses. Pictured with TCSC Director Patricia Peterson is Buck Hill's General Manager, Dick Lempke and Race Coordinator, Gabe Cyr.

At the Annual Shareholders Meeting on November 13, 1985, Chuck told those present that the ski business had not been good these first five seasons in the 80's. Insurance and utility costs have been increasing at abnormal rates. There have been big increases in fixed costs, while income remains stable. He also spoke of government supported ski areas versus private areas and indicated that competition

Dave and Barb Evenson, owners of the SKI CHALLENGE.

becomes fierce when government dollars are expended for ski area operations and improvements.

On October 17, 1986, Chuck wrote a letter to Governor Perpich in which he expressed his concerns about the major issues facing the ski industry in Minnesota, namely the liability insurance problem and the development of ski facilities by government agencies within the state:

Historically, skiing is a recreational endeavor that has always been served by the private sector, as it has been able to fulfill the skier needs and increase capacity to insure growth. To my knowledge, the only 3 ski areas in the U.S. built since the 50's with government monies are all in the state of Minnesota. Hyland Hills, Giant's Ridge, and Spirit Mountain were all constructed and improved while the (capacity) needs of the skier were already being met by the private sector, and there was an excess of capacity within the state. During this same time period, in fact, seven areas have gone out of business and two others are managed by banks as they were unable to meet their financial commitments. I do feel Hyland Hills had a huge impact on Ski Tonka and Cedar Hills closing down. Spirit Mountain was a major problem for Tony Wise at Mount Telemark.

Governor Perpich replied to Chuck, in a letter dated December 26, 1986. He defended the government involvement in the ski industry and suggested he (Chuck) contact the tourism director with his concerns.

The private ski areas in Minnesota became more and more concerned about the unfair competition that the government endowed ski areas were exhibiting, such as lower ticket and season pass prices. Another new benefit concerning the government's assistance to Giant's Ridge was a new, four lane highway to the area. In January of 1987, Phil Peterson, president of the Twin City Independent Ski Areas Association, wrote a letter to Mr. Hank Todd, director of tourism, expressing concerns about the government in the ski business. Another example of the concern of government support was a 1987 letter from the Quadna Mt. Employee Committee:

One final and very important issue that hasn't been addressed, is the issue of Giant's Ridge at Biwabik. Nine million state dollars had already been spent on the area. Now Governor Perpich is proposing to put another thirteen million taxpayer dollars in the area. Wouldn't those twenty plus million dollars be put to better use supporting the privately owned resorts and recreational areas in the state? The employees at Quadna strongly feel the politicians have sold them all short. It is time that they wake up and take a good look at what is happening.

Quadna Mountain (the largest taxpayer and employer in Aitken County), and Sugar Hills went out of business shortly after this letter was written. What better served the taxpayers of Minnesota – having a business fail that greatly supported a county or pouring millions of tax dollars into businesses that could not generate a profit, even with state aid?

Two years later Chuck was still very concerned about the ongoing competition between state sponsored ski areas and private ski areas. In June of 1988, the Iron Range Resource and Rehabilitation Board reported that Giant's Ridge had lost two million dollars that year. If it weren't for its dedicated employees, it would have been very difficult for the private areas to compete with the government run ski areas. Chuck explained his concern in a letter to the shareholders in 1988:

> ...by far, the biggest problem facing our industry in this state, is the unusual involvement of the State of Minnesota in the ski business. It is extremely difficult to compete with areas whose facilities were built with tax dollars, pay no property taxes, and their losses are subsidized by the taxpayers. This trend is frightening and these areas have become extremely aggressive in pricing their product for the skier. At the three public areas in our state, (Spirit Mountain, Duluth, Giants Ridge, Hibbing, and Hyland Hills, Bloomington) over 28 million dollars have been spent on ski facilities, when there was (already) an excess of capacity provided by the private sector.

At the 1986 shareholders' meeting, Chuck reported that the 1985-86 season was a good snow year and gross receipts were up at both areas. The major accomplishment at Buck Hill that year was the acquisition of the Walsh property, which was 29 acres to the north of Buck Hill. We also purchased the Buck Hill property that St. Olaf owned (which had been left to St. Olaf upon Grace Whittier's death), leaving Buck Hill a total of 82 acres. Liability insurance remained a problem and property insurance increased 15%. This state sponsorship of competing ski areas continued to be an ongoing concern for local ski areas.

Beginning in the late 1980's, the growth of the surrounding suburbs contributed to the growth of Buck Hill. We began expanding our ski school programs and high school racing programs, as well as the group business. Among the many large groups who skied at Buck Hill were ski clubs from many of the nearby junior and senior high schools. Each of the school groups took lessons and skied at Buck Hill once a week. There were about 300 students participating each afternoon and they also returned for free skiing. This was a very popular program.

Dick Strand was happy to be back on the slopes.

In the winter of 86-87, Chuck and board member, Dick Strand, put on their chef hats and brought back the Sunday brunch. It was held in the Bucket Hillside Room and turned out to be quite a popular event. The two of them really enjoyed cooking together and they were both members of the Amateur Chefs Society (a local group of men that liked to get together and cook and which I believe is still around today). Here are some favorite recipes forwarded to me from Dick Strand:

Joe's Special (an old, San Francisco Concoction)

> 1 ½ lbs. hamburger
> 3T chopped onions
> 1 package frozen spinach
> 3 eggs
> 3 T Olive Oil

Preheat the skillet with the olive oil. Break up the meat in the pan and keep it separated. Add the onions. Add the spinach (precooked and drained), Keep working the ingredients with a long handled fork. When meat appears done, fork in the three eggs, right from the shells. Spatula it up on to plates – Serve with a generous amount of ketchup.

(From "Hippo Cookbook", copyright 1969 Tex Jack Falvey/Pacific Productions)

Hotel Anderson Apple Pancakes (Hurry-up Jones version)
Served for breakfast every day at the Hotel Anderson in Wabasha, MN

> A package of pancake mix
> 1 T cooking oil
> ½ apple chopped fine
> 1/8 t. cinnamon
> few grains of nutmeg
> 1 egg, beaten

Follow the directions on the package for a standard batch of pancakes. Then add 1 T cooking oil, 1 beaten egg and the chopped apple and spices. Bake on a hot, lightly greased griddle. Serve with butter and sugar. Makes about 16 pancakes. Then hit the slopes!

(From "500 Recipes by Request" by Jeane M. Hall and Belle Anderson Ebner)

Another original event at Buck Hill was the very first Law Enforcement Ski Championship in March of 1987. The slalom shootout was won by Craig Norby, a patrolman of the Minneapolis 5th Precinct. Lt. Gaylord Gladwin, of the same unit, was runner-up for overall honors and first in the over 50's class. There were winners in all age groups including 70 to 80 year old retired police officers. When the National Association of Police Skiers Race was held in Snowmass, Colorado,

Minnesota sent the largest contingent of 30 skiers.

In the *St. Cloud Times* on November 26, 1988, Dave Price wrote an article about Powder Ridge manager, Jerry Wahlin:

MINNESOTA PEACE OFFICERS SKI ASSOCIATION "Medal Winners" at the 1989 National Peace Officers Ski Race in Snowmass, Colorado.

Gaylord and the police officers race.

Jerry Wahlin, manager at Powder Ridge, is happy when it snows because it makes people think about winter activities – skiing for instance. The fact that the white stuff covers the 12 slopes at the area is almost an incidental benefit. Powder Ridge has been open since Wednesday, due in large part to its snow-making equipment. Despite the hectic pace of operating a ski area during the winter, even the boss finds time to get out on the slopes occasionally. Shortly after lunchtime on Friday, Wahlin was out skiing with his daughters, Samantha and Andrea. At age one, Samantha isn't quite ready to strap on skis yet, but she seemed very happy as her dad held her and gently glided down the bunny hill. On the other hand, Andrea, who's nearly three, wore both her skis and the determined look of a future champion.

At the Annual shareholders meeting on November 14, 1989, Chuck indicated that the last winter season of 1988-89 had been excellent. Gross sales were up 17% and Buck Hill had the best gross receipts ever. Dick Lempke reported that this past summer, snow-making had been expanded and the Bucket had been remodeled.

Jerry Wahlin reported that, "The past season has also been excellent and there has already been an increase in season pass sales this fall. New for this season is expansion of the snow-making system and new rental equipment has been purchased." After much consideration (wringing of hands and gnashing of teeth) it was decided that Powder Ridge would allow snowboarding and it turned out to be a good decision.

Chuck reported on the ongoing discussions we were having with the City of Burnsville. The concept would be a sale and lease-back program of the ski area and the purchase would be backed by General Obligation Bonds or Revenue

Bonds. The City had approached Dakota County relative to its interest in the purchase and the city would also have to get approval from the Metropolitan Council. After a number of meetings, the whole idea simply drifted away.

Although vandalism had always been a problem at Buck Hill, it seemed to intensify in the late 80's and early 90's. The vandals would break the windows in the lift houses and destroy the control panels. A favorite target were the lights on the hill for rock throwing practice. Another problem was graffiti that often named their favorite political candidates, which I did not necessarily always agree with, making it all the more frustrating. Not only was it expensive to fix the damage, but also very time consuming for the employees. Another problem we have had at the area was the theft of skis and snowboards. Yes, this is sad, but to deal with this we installed a free equipment checking area and we also had paid police officers on the premises most of the time. This move definitely helped alleviate a lot of the problem.

1996, snowmaking at Buck Hill. Or is it the return of the Glacial Age?

THE NINETIES

Snowboarding, Freestyle Team, Chuck Stone, Mountain Biking, Burnsville Business, Don McClure, Wind Chill, Powder Ridge Expansion, New Years Eve, Tubing, Olympians, Bed Race for Bridging, Major Improvements, and Gabe Cyr

In the summer of 1996, a 12,000 square foot addition to the chalet at Powder Ridge.

Early in 1990, Chuck wrote a summary of all the ideas he hoped could be implemented at the two ski areas. I know he was frustrated, as the plans he had talked about for so many years were not being taken seriously. He wrote to the board, "I would hope at our next meetings we could generate some discussions and possibly implement some new ideas which might increase our skier visits. I think we have to establish some new goals and redo our game plan. The starting point might be the 40 suggestions which I presented last March. Perhaps they are all lousy suggestions, but at least it would be a point at which to start."

A few items from his wish list (of 40) included:
- Not only would I allow snowboarding, I would include a half-pipe and a snow- board park.
- Build a children's terrain garden on Skunk Hollow or the J-Bar area.
- Library.
- Increase ski patrol and instructor's family passes.
- Light up our fences, similar to Sun Valley.
- Bring back the Sunday Brunch.
- Do more inter-area advertising.
- Bigger effort to sell gift certificates at Christmas time.
- Update the bathrooms.
- Keep the Bucket and Bar open year round.

I am pleased to report that all of the above were eventually accomplished. I even started a library. I must say it is still quite primitive at this point but I have high hopes that it will eventually have a proper place at the area. Other ideas that he talked about at that time were miniature golf, a Halloween haunt, and a resort hotel on the north property. We did give Halloween a whirl in 2009, but the others are still in the possible future stage.

Pierce* Skate and Ski held an October Fest preview party at Buck Hill on October 4, 1990. It was a chance to meet Olympic Gold medalist, Stein Eriksen, and former U.S. Ski Team members, Andy Mill, Pam Fletcher, and the Pierce Pro staff. Festivities included live music by Chuck Hinz, ski movies, food and drinks, and door prizes. The event was successful and it was a good preview of what was new in equipment and clothing for the upcoming season.

On November 16, 1990 Chuck reported to the shareholders: "We have made some changes at both areas for the coming season. You might have read in the newspaper that Buck Hill had considerable flood damage due to the rupture of a main water line in Burnsville. Burnsville's insurance company was very accommodating and because of the water damage, carpeting was replaced in the main chalet, several snow guns' electrical apparatus, one ski lift's low voltage wiring, and control panel were all replaced and a little over 1,000 yards of gravel was hauled in to repair the parking lot. This will be the first winter of snowboarding at Buck Hill. Both ski areas are in top notch condition and we are anticipating a banner season."

A colorful view of Mont Le Buc.

Chuck Stone, Pete Ankeny, Jack Taylor, and Dave Cost, good friends taking some runs at Snowmass.

The Stones taking some runs at Vail.

In a letter to the shareholders on November 22, 1991, Chuck had some very good news: "We are off to a tremendous start at Buck Hill this year and opened October 31st due to the record breaking Halloween snowstorm which totaled 28.4 inches of snow. The area has been busy for the past three weeks and we are hopeful that this will be a very successful season." Jerry reported that Powder Ridge had opened November 9th. He noted that "...expansion progress was ongoing during the summer. The ponding area was built and lined with clay and the new pump system doubled the snowmaking capacity. Next year we will begin moving dirt, and a new chairlift will be added. Season pass sales to this date are better than any time in Powder Ridges history." Jerry added that the "Star of the North Games" would be held at the area in mid-January 1992.

Early in 1992, we were informed that the retail giant, Walmart, was in the process of looking for land in Burnsville and foremost on their list was the corner of Buck Hill Road and Crystal Lake Road. Obviously, this would cause all kinds of problems for the ski area, known and unknown. Most importantly, there would be increased traffic and loss of aesthetic value. Who wants to ski right next to a Walmart and its trucks? Chuck wrote a letter to the Burnsville Planning Commission, on June 8, 1992 addressing his concerns, not the least of which is having a huge, retail complex just down the road. He tried to stress the value Buck Hill has contributed to the surrounding area. "A ski area is an irreplaceable asset for your community. The quality of life is enhanced in Burnsville because we offer wholesome recreation for thousands of people. Buck Hill employs over 400 people and 90% of them are young men and women. We accommodate the local high schools' ski teams as well as running weekly and regional Lake Conference ski meets." The letter continued with many more reasons why Buck Hill's future is an important consideration in making this decision. Walmart did eventually find suitable property just south of the Minnesota River.

Chuck summed up our accomplishments for '92 in a letter to the shareholders in December:

> For the past 37 years Buck Hill, Inc. has fostered the belief that people of all ages are eager to enjoy the experience of alpine skiing. Through the years, the ski industry has grown more complex, but the basic appeals and rewards of skiing have not changed. Successfully keeping pace with the challenge of change has kept Buck Hill on the leading edge of the recreational skiing industry. Over this period, we have acquired 160 acres of valuable property, installed seven chairlifts and six surface lifts, developed our base complexes, snowmaking, lighting, etc. We look forward to the challenge of the '90s and hope to continue our growth pattern.

At Powder Ridge, the three-year expansion program had been completed. This included a 4,000 square foot addition to the chalet, a snowmaking pond,

Chuck checking out the new Quad at Powder Ridge

Load testing the new Quad at Powder Ridge.

additional snowmaking capacity, additional lights, a hill buildup and a new quad chairlift. I personally feel that now Powder Ridge is a very competitive Midwest ski area and I hope all of you will take time to see the facility.

Hill buildup at Powder Ridge - a major improvement.

The Buck Hill Freestyle team had some major accomplishments in 1993, representing the Central Division at the Junior National Freestyle Championships March 11-13 in Salt Lake City, Utah. Medalists were Jason Schulberg of Prior Lake, men 17-18, Jackie Carlson of Prior Lake, women 17-18, and Jonathan Kirkwood of Apple Valley, boys 15-16. Other Buck Hill freestyle team members who represented the Central Division were Dan Johnson, Dave Johnson, and Jim Winebarger of Lakeville; Shawn Eggleston and Dave Kline of Apple Valley; Mark Olson of Burnsville; Scott Hebeisen and Jon Kobs of Excelsior.

The team was coached by Ken Zylstra of Prior Lake and Pat Menning of Burnsville. In addition, Schulberg, Kirkwood, and Hebeisen had qualified for the Senior National Championships that were held in April at Breckenridge, Colorado. They competed with Olympic and World Cup team members as well as other top U.S. freestyle skiers.

Pacesetters: Julian Kuz, Chip Burhans, Craig Jennings, Jim Holst, 1990's

NASTAR continued to be

90

very strong at Buck Hill. A younger Buck Hill racer, Nelson Carlson, who raced NASTAR and was also on the Buck Hill Ski Racing Team, was mentioned in the December 1994 issue of *Ski Magazine*. Nelson at age 9 scored the lowest NASTAR handicap in the Boys' 7-9 age group for the 1993-1994 season in the country.

Modern snowboarding began in 1965 when Sherman Poppen bolted two children's skis together. His wife Nancy called it the Snurfer for snow and surfing. Other enthusiasts came on board (pun intended) and Jake Burton designed a binding to attach to the board and made other modifications. Snowboarding became more popular in the 70's and 80's. Ski areas adopted the sport very slowly and at first there was some animosity between skiers and snowboarders. In 1985, only 7% of U.S. ski areas allowed boarding. By 1990, some ski areas had separate slopes for the boarders with rails and half pipes. There were a few hold-outs, but most areas allowed snowboarding by the mid-90's. Powder Ridge welcomed snowboarders for the 1991-1992 season and Buck Hill did the next year. There were very few problems between the two sports at our areas. By the 2009-2010 season there were 8.2 million snowboarders in the United States and growth tended to level off after that.

At a shareholders' meeting in 1992, Dick Lempke talked about snowboarding for the current season and how it would affect our patronage and other problems that might occur. At the time, there was a lot of bad press about snowboarding. Although popular, it had attracted a lot of attention because of accidents that were occurring between snowboarders and skiers. He said the jury was still out about its future and coexisting with downhill skiers. After much discussion, and based on snowboarding's success at Powder Ridge, the board decided to allow snowboarding at Buck Hill in the '92-'93 season. It proved to be a wise decision.

In the same meeting in '92, Chuck reported that the previous year Buck Hill had an excellent November followed by a disappointing remainder of the season. He also said that an addition to the Hutch would offer another room with a fireplace for groups with a fireplace for groups

Boardercross became a very popular event.

and clubs. Tony Anthonisen was hired as marketing director in mid August of 1992. Tony achieved some lofty results in his first year which included 136% increase in Boy Scout bookings and 98% increase in all other group bookings. Tony had many other useful innovative marketing ideas that were very successful and still used to this day.

In the early nineties, John and Betsy Massie became owners of the Skijammers, one of the roving ski schools which we welcomed at both areas. The Massie's wrote:

> There were more than 1,250 children enrolled in the program during our years of ownership. We always found Buck Hill to be very friendly and accommodating. All of our preseason training for our instructors were run at Buck Hill in December. There were a lot of night clinics leading up to the Saturday Skijammers Academy. We added a night race program called Teamjammers, and a certification program for our instructors. Don McClure always gave us hill space to train on and indoor space for meetings. Bottom line, Buck Hill was and is a great partner for Skijammers. We feel this relationship has benefited both parties involved. We appreciated all that Buck Hill has done for us and the ski school industry. Many kids are life-long skiers because of it! Thanks.

The early nineties were not a very positive period for Buck Hill. There were numerous complaints about the direction Buck Hill was going. They included uncaring employees, lack of promoting the area, and a very disgruntled freestyle team as the terrain they used had to be re-contoured for snowboarding. Chuck was also quite disturbed because so many of his ideas were not being implemented and he was acutely aware of the atmosphere at Buck Hill. He believed that you

Dick Howell, board member since 1960.

must provide a positive and caring environment because, after all, the public is there to have fun. Management seemed happy with the status quo and Chuck desperately wanted some new ideas to be put in place. He wanted a better attitude, beginning at the top, to trickle down to the employees. The health of the business was a top concern, but so was the happiness and satisfaction of the employees and Buck Hill's guests. Chuck was never satisfied unless new ideas were being tried. This was not the situation at Powder Ridge where the business was in a very good place.

A year later, at the spring of 1993 board meeting, Chuck reported that Powder Ridge's performance for the 92-93 season was the best in its history. Dick Howell[*] and Dick Strand gave a report on options to expand Buck Hill which were snow tubing and a sports bar. Numerous meetings had been held with the owners of the Village Inn, a successful sports bar in St. Paul. These owners were very encouraging about the business. A motion was made to continue to explore a joint venture with the Village Inn. This idea did not come to fruition.

One of the last letters Chuck wrote was on December 19, 1993 to Dick Lempke, Buck Hill's manager. As always, he was very concerned about the coming season. The last paragraph read, "Although the results through November are not too promising, and I realize the weather has not been accommodating, I feel we must remain very positive. I believe that during the course of the season things tend to level out and usually an area can make up for a bad start. If we do a good job making snow and fulfilling the needs of our skiing guests, we can remain prosperous." I think this final letter is a great example of Chuck's never-ending enthusiasm and optimism. That quality, more than anything else, had much to do with the overall success of Buck Hill and Powder Ridge.

It was a very sad beginning for 1994, as Chuck passed away on January 7th, after a very short illness (remarkably, he had played tennis with Jessica and skied the previous week). Gabe Cyr, Buck Hill racing coordinator hired by Chuck 17 years prior said, "We're going to miss him something terrible. He knew what

he was doing. He was the best friend the skier ever had." Of course this made a huge impact on my life and I almost immediately decided that, under the circumstances, I would not want to be involved with Buck Hill. I went so far as to tell the board that I wished to sell my stock in the company. This was a very unsettling time for me and my family, and the ski areas as well. But, as winter went on, I found I could not stay away from Buck Hill and I became a little more involved in the business. I had been ordering hats, mittens, gloves, pins and other items for our small accessory shop in the ticket office since 1954 and I continued to do that. I was very aware about how the season was going and I heard complaints from some of the employees as I came to spend more time at the area.

At the board meeting in February, 1994, I made a motion to appoint Stuart Campbell and Tom Warner to return to the board as directors and that was approved. I was elected Chairman of the Board and Stuart became president. I received quite a few letters from board members

40th Anniversary brochure features our first poster from 1954. Designed by Marea Campbell.

who gave me a vote of confidence and for that I was thankful. Dick Lempke reported on the financial situation at both areas and both were quite a bit behind last season's cash flow in operations. A long discussion followed on how we might improve the situation in the middle of the season. Both areas became computerized in 1994.

We discussed the pros and cons of mountain biking and we decided to go ahead with the plan for more mountain bike trails. Jim Holst was in charge of the program. Jim made a very good case for Buck Hill to become more involved in mountain biking. He argued in a presentation to the board: "Buck Hill has already been the site for the second largest mountain bike race in the Midwest for the past few years. It's reputation for a fun and challenging course is already well known. Tour De Buck has drawn racers from Hawaii, Colorado, Illinois, North and South Dakota, as well as other adjacent states and local riders. With the trail options already in place, the course has been different all 5 years." The Annual Tour De Buck event was scheduled for Sunday, August 7th, 1994 and promised to be a spectacular race.

We developed a very congenial relationship with Pat Sorenson of Penn Cycle that had begun in 1991. Penn Cycle had a Thursday night race series that is still very popular to this day. There was always a blizzard of bikers that showed up to participate in a myriad of events.

Mountain biking at Buck Hill.

94

REI Tour De Buck biking race was held again in August of 1995 and a spokesman for REI commented to us about the success of the race: "With 345 racers, the Tour de Buck was by far the biggest race of the Midwest Series this year! We estimate an equal number of spectators took in the action as well. Thanks so much for your generous support in making Buck Hill available for the race. Your cooperation was a key factor in making the race the overwhelming success that it was."

It is important to note that the Buck Hill employee manual of 1995 contained all the information an employee might need to know in the way of benefits, attire, rules and regulations. It firmly stated that the employee could wear "no more than 3 earrings per ear." I guess there were no restrictions on nose decorations!

Don McClure began working with Al Werthauser, founder of Aljohn's Beach and Boards, about the snowboard park we intended to build at Buck Hill. Snowboarding was growing at a rapid pace and working with Al turned out to be beneficial to both parties. Aljohns did a terrific job of promoting snowboarding with special events at the area. There were always lots of participants, live music, great prizes and a good time. Snowboarding was in its infancy at Buck Hill and it was very popular.

The snowboard park was very popular.

In the spring of 1995, it was apparent that there were many problems facing Buck Hill, the most compelling was our financial position. We engaged a new accounting firm at this time, Larson, Allen & Weishar. Then, the City of Burnsville stated that they were going to build a new road (Greenhaven Drive) that would run east to west on the north boundary of our property which divided it into three parcels, which was not to our advantage whatsoever. The road was to serve surrounding apartments, and did not benefit Buck Hill in the least. Walter Bush, Tom Warner, and I met with Bob Hoffman at Larkin, Hoffman, Daly and Lindgren to consult on how to proceed. Bob had worked with us on the "Stopping Walmart" Project.

Peter Coyle became the attorney on the project and he guided us on the city's land acquisition proposal (2.1 acres). There were also special assessments charged to us which we felt were excessively high! We filed an "Objection to Special Assessments for Buck Hill Road Improvements" as it was clear that the proposed assessments of $265,476.92, bore no reasonable relationship to any benefits that might be received by Buck Hill. After a number of meetings with attorneys and the city, an agreement was reached in November of 1995. A sum of $210,000 was paid to Buck Hill for the 2.1 acres and the right of way. The assessments of $149,604 to us on the undeveloped property were deferred until 2001 unless development took place. We considered this a fair and reasonable settlement.

In addition to the Greenhaven problem, there were many other current issues which were very important to Buck Hill's future. These included the broadcast antennas proposed by KSTP, zoning and the gas line under the property. The chalet could never be expanded due to the line unless the pipe was moved, which would be a huge expense.

We had considered selling the Walsh property to help alleviate some of our cash problems. We began negotiations with Sun Tide Realty to investigate a possible partnership with them. Gary and Eric Gabrielson, officers of Sun Tide, gave a presentation regarding the future development of Buck Hill. They talked about bringing in equity

Nancy Stone with her grandchildren in 1995 - Jenny and Emily Stone, Max and Madeline Wiltgen.

partners with the current shareholders and building 75 apartment units, 25,000 feet of retail outlet stores, restaurants and a recreational area. Pulte Homes was also interested in buying the Walsh property. We ended up not selling at that time, and decided to see how business progressed.

At the July 19, 1995 board meeting, I was elected president of the corporation along with my other duties as treasurer and CEO.

The 1995-96 season opened on November 10th, two weeks earlier than the previous year. The winter season of 1994-1995 had not gone well but we were very optimistic about the upcoming year.

Some significant changes had been made in the previous few months. Dick Lempke had resigned and Don McClure became the new general manager. He had been at the area

BMX - Bicycle Motor Cross

since 1975 when he was on the ski patrol and he was familiar with every aspect of the ski business. Mark Mitchelette was the new controller and Jessica (Stone) Wiltgen was the new marketing director. Marie Lambader continued as secretary and George Kukucka continued as supervisor of food operations. Our son Charles also came on board at that time. He did some accounting, kept registers current, worked in the cash room, the ticket office, and the food service. He also helped me with some office work and there are many of his photographs in this history as well. Terry Pankratz came to Buck Hill about this time. He was a lift supervisor but also helped with other outside duties. Gary Davis became the new rental shop manager. The mountain biking program under the guidance of Jim Holst had grown rapidly the previous summer.

Another development that summer was that KSTP (Hubbard Broadcasting) had installed a tower cam on the top of the hill. We had an agreement that they could not talk about wind chill, but they could talk about the great skiing they saw below! We felt that this arrangement would provide some very good publicity for Buck Hill, and the sport of skiing as well. We did not charge KSTP for this arrangement and it has been beneficial to both of us and still is.

Charles Stone III at one of his many stations, 2008

One more comment about the ongoing problem of wind-chill came from Phil Peterson of MnSNO, an organization of ski areas and shops that were bound together to promote the ski and snowboard industry. Phil wrote, "Wind chill is here to stay and... get worse. Real temperatures are a thing of the past. Rules are now based on wind-chill. We have never seen school cancellations to this degree and for the first time, we are even seeing school ski teams cancel practices due to, yup, you guessed it, wind chill."

Walter Bush and daughter Anne Bush Hanson, happy to be skiing.

During 1995 and 1996, we had conversations with Burnsville city officials and Dakota County about the possibility of Burnsville buying the area and Buck Hill would have a management contract. After several discussions the idea was abandoned. Gregg Eppich joined the staff in 1996 at Buck Hill as our new comptroller.

Tyler and Weston Traub on their first day of skiing at Buck Hill.

Don and The Pipe Dragon, 1998.

Gregg Eppich, new comptroller

Walter Bush resigned his post as secretary after 42 years but he remained on the board. We all agreed that Walter provided invaluable legal services to the corporation and has added to the success of Buck Hill since the very beginning. Walter's nickname for the area was Mont Le Buc. Colby Lund took over as secretary. At that time Colby, an attorney in Minneapolis was the assistant program director of the Buck Hill Ski Racing team and had been a coach with the team since 1979.

It was an exciting beginning for two future Buck Hill racers in 1996, when these young boys had their first day of skiing. Their father, Tom Traub, described the event:

It was winter of 1996. Tyler was 5 years old and Weston would have just turned 4 years old. We put them in lessons in the morning and after lunch we took them up on the triple chair. Once Wes was pointed downhill he went straight down Teachers Pet and might have skied into the Hutch Chalet if Holly hadn't yelled at me to stop him. At about 15 paces from the chalet, I caught up with Wes, picked him up and came to a stop before we crashed into the building. Meanwhile, Tyler was carving good turns down the hill the way he was taught in lessons that morning. Both boys skied in the Buck Hill junior racing program and also were members of the 2008 Lakeville North High School State Championship Alpine Ski Team.

Jessica reported on the marketing plan for the upcoming winter season. It would include radio spots, newspaper ads, billboards and television commercials. We had installed a billboard for the first time and the area had developed a web site, SKIBUCK.COM. Snowboarding had made a significant impact at all of the areas nationwide. Nationally, snowboarders made up approximately 14% of the 53.1 million visits in 1995-96. They represented almost 20% of Buck Hill's business. We had excellent facilities at both areas, specifically designed for the boarder. Creating terrain specifically for snowboarders helped alleviate potential encounters with skiers.

We added 10-new HKD Tower snow guns to Milk Run. These state of the art snow guns were 90% more efficient than the previous guns and reduced electrical consumption while they increased production rates significantly. The Pipe Dragon was purchased, which was an ingenious piece of equipment that constructed a half pipe for snowboarders.

Many of our customers often asked why the exit to Buck Hill off of Highway 35W was not marked more clearly, (as the Minnesota Zoo, and others were). I wrote a letter to Governor Arne Carlson in 1996:

October 3, 1996

Dear Governor Carlson,

I am writing to you in regard to a long standing signage problem we have at Buck Hill Ski Area in Burnsville. Buck Hill has been operating here in Burnsville for 42 years, long before the construction of Highway 35W. Since that time in 1954, when Buck Hill first opened for business, we have seen highway exit signs appear for the Minnesota Zoo, Canterbury Downs, Murphy's Landing, and the Mystic Lake Casino. Over the years many of our customers have asked the unanswerable question, where are the exit signs for the ski area?

Buck Hill is considered a Dakota County landmark and has been for hundreds of years. In addition to our skiing operation, we are now open all year with mountain biking and other summer related business's. I certainly hope that you would agree that skiing is more important to the quality of life in Minnesota than gambling. A new major highway County Road 46 is currently being constructed just south of Buck Hill and will also need exit signs for the ski area. I look forward to hearing from you on this very important matter to Buck Hill.

Yours truly,

Nancy Stone
President, Buck Hill, Inc.

New entrance sign.

I cannot find Governor Carlson's reply, if there was one. However, we did get ski area signs on County Road 42 and 46 for the Buck Hill road very soon after this letter was sent! The reason that we did is because Don McClure and Jason Schulberg, on our behalf, bought two signs indicating a ski area and put them up themselves. It was one way to get things done and the signs are still there today.

At Powder Ridge in the summer of 1996, a large, two story, 12,000 square foot (60x80) addition was added to the north end of the chalet. The upper level became known as the North Chalet and had seating capacity for approximately 340 people. The new addition included a lounge area known as Chester's, which served a large variety of beverages and food. The name Chester came from our family dog. Chuck often took him, a collie mix and as gentle as they come, to Powder Ridge on his weekend visits. Chester would roam around the chalet to be petted, and he would also enjoy a snack now and then from his younger friends. I don't think he knew how to growl or bark.

Chester, devoted fan of Powder Ridge

Buck Hill and Powder Ridge employees were always coming up with new ideas to enhance the experience of its customers. Even though Powder Ridge had a very popular New Year's Eve party, Buck Hill did not. Don loved fireworks, (recently licensed) and was all fired up about the possibility of exploding them at Buck Hill.

New Year's Eve soon became an annual tradition and one of Buck Hill's best skier/snowboarder visitor days. Don would handle the fireworks outside and Jessica would handle the entertainment inside. There was always a big band in the Whittier room, Jeff Wiltgen was the lead singer in a popular local band called The Rhythm Junkies, and the band ended up playing for 16 straight years at the area. Other entertainment included: Erik the Juggling Magician, Kevin Hall's Magic Show (A semi-finalist on America's Got talent), a torchlight parade, clowns, and in the beginning,

New Year's Eve fireworks

childcare. We also provided what we called Glitter-Glam-Hair-do's. Basically, kids would get their hair done for free. The hair-do's included lots of colored hair spray, blinky lights, pony tails, and glitter. Our Granddaughter's Madeline Wiltgen and Emily Stone, both worked a few times in the booth doing hair-dos.

"Support Our Troops Day" was held twice a year in which military families could ski, snowboard, or tube free and they were given the Hutch Chalet in which to meet, greet, and eat. It was usually very well attended. It seemed like the least we could do.

In February of 1997, Bob Hammond visited Buck Hill and wrote an article in the *Minneapolis Star Tribune* about what was happening on a typical afternoon at Buck Hill in the middle of the winter. The article also illustrated how diversified the ski business had become. During his visit, in the lower Bucket, Terri Pierce of Pierce Skate and Ski was showing the ladies the latest in goggles, sunscreen, ski-tuning devices, etc. Buck Hill always had a very cordial relationship with the Pierces who had established a first rate skate and ski shop in Bloomington in 1936. Hammond wrote:

> Upstairs in the Sports Bucket, a co-ed group that was much larger and noisier than the ladies downstairs, was milling about, getting some last minute instructions and strapping on numbered bibs before heading to a giant slalom race course. They were members of the Ski Challenge, a not-too-serious race league with team names such as Wapid Wacers, Team Dirtbag, Bums Away, Ladies of the Night, and Blazing Saddlebags.

Ski Challenge racers warming up for the big event.

A handicapped system allowed neophyte snowplowers to race alongside Olympic wanna-be's and all ages were welcome.

I headed outside and hopped on a chairlift. Halfway up the hill I caught sight of a train of about six little kids snaking down Ballroom, Buck's most popular intermediate trail. The locomotive was a Buck Hill instructor, leading a SKIwee class of preschoolers. They get lessons and a snack, play games, and go home with a progress card. Meanwhile, on the south end of the ski area, snowboarders were using a rope tow to access special terrain carved out for them including jumps, ramps and curvy ravines. Sleepy ski area? Hardly. Here's the moral: Take a good hard look at your local ski hill. There's probably more going on than you ever imagined.

In the annual report to the shareholders in the fall of 1997, Jerry reported that that gross sales at Powder Ridge during the '96-'97 season were the best in its history. Snowboarding continued to grow and sales in the new Chester's Lounge were steadily increasing.

At this time, we were contemplating some additions to Buck Hill, one of which was a tubing area. We wanted to expand group sales and tubing would offer something for everyone in the winter. We would delay the opening until 3:00 P.M. on week-ends to help alleviate our parking problems. Buck Hill was also exploring the possibility of an addition to the Bucket or the main chalet as we desperately needed the space! Don contacted the city about our tubing project on four acres of our own property as we would need to remove some trees. A four-page letter came back with all the ground rules and we were required to post a bond of $52,500.

We officially terminated our discussions with Pulte Homes as business was good and we decided to keep the property rather than sell. As I look back at that period, I am very thankful we did not sell any property or the ski area at that time. There were other proposals, some of which were to the point of ridiculous. One board member offered me an undervalued price for my stock in the company, which I did not accept. Phew! From 1995-1997, both areas made great strides in their financial position. I pitched in the next few summers and went back to doing some outside painting. I also followed in Chuck's footsteps by updating the Buck Hill Racing Team gallery on the east wall of the main chalet and new pictures in the fireplace room.

At the April 23, 1998 board meeting, I reported that some interested board members and I had met with Tim Olinger of Miller Architects/Builders on Monday, April 13th to discuss a proposal made by them for construction of a new chalet. Our financial position was strong so we decided to go ahead with the project or more accurately, a remodeling of the Bucket with a major addition, which was completed in 2001.

In the fall of 1998, the anticipated "Wild Chutes Snow Tubing Park" at Powder Ridge became a reality. It opened during the 1998-1999 season with four 15-foot-wide lanes of controlled tubing with lights for night tubing and quickly

became very popular with customers. Also at Powder Ridge, the management team wanted more ownership in the company and most board members thought it was a good idea. We decided to look into the possibility of spinning off Powder Ridge.

In the annual report to the shareholders in the fall of 1998, I wrote, "That although the winter of 1997-1998 was the second warmest of the century, both Powder

Family fun on the tubing hill at Powder Ridge.

Ridge and Buck Hill managed to increase gross receipts." The book value per share of Buck Hill, Inc. had increased 42% in three years. Don added: "This past summer was a busy one at Buck Hill with the construction of a new tubing hill and the re-grading of Sleepy Hollow. We are extremely excited about these two new improvements. The re-grading has added more racing terrain and will allow us to book additional high school race teams for week night practices. The financial projections for both areas look promising."

In addition, I wrote, "We are immensely proud of our two Olympians, Kristina Koznick and Tasha Nelson, who raced in Nagano, Japan in February of 1998. They joined Joe Levin who had raced in the 1992 Olympics in Albertville, France." Our racing program director, Erich Sailer, was the recipient of three very prestigious awards this year, the United States Ski Association Domestic Coach of the Year, the USSA Development Team Coach of the Year and United States Olympic Committee Development Coach of the Year. He received these awards at a ceremony in Park City, Utah. This is the first year the USOC named a Coach of the Year in skiing, and that person was Erich. We all congratulated him on these honors.

Bob Beattie, host of of ESPN's weekly show, *Ski World* came to Buck Hill on January of 1999. Gregg Wong wrote about the event in the *St. Paul Pioneer Press*, January 13, 1999:

Aspen. Vail. Sun Valley. Jackson Hole. Deer Valley. Park City. St. Anton. Kitzbuhel. Bob Beattie is visiting them all this ski season for his

ESPN television program, *Ski World*, which is in its 13th year." Beattie said that he had wanted to do a show from Buck Hill for a long time. Wong quoted Beattie in his article saying, "I've always liked the place; I'm from New Hampshire and grew up on hills like this. I always have a great time on small hills." Beattie selected Buck Hill as one of 14 locations for *Ski World* installments, largely because Buck Hill had produced so many standout ski racers.

ESPN's Bob Beattie, left, interviews members of Bloomington Kennedy's ski team while doing a feature on Buck Hill

I was thrilled with the plan that the area was going to be featured on national television. I thought that Buck Hill deserved the recognition. We had done a lot for skiing over the years. Of course, Erich Sailer also had a lot to do with that. I would like to add that Gregg Wong had contributed a great deal to the success of the ski business in Minnesota. His articles were always accurate, informative, interesting, and fun. All Minnesota ski areas have benefited from Gregg Wongs knowledge of the ski business.

There were many memorable charitable events over the years, one of

Could this really be the band KISS at Buck Hill?

Bed Races - The Wizard of Oz crew

Greek Goddesses at the 2003 Bed Race

Clowning around at the Bed Race in 2011

Bedbugs at Bed Race for Bridging, 2011 - Tracy Hemeon, Jess Geisinger, Nancy Stone, Amanda Davis, and Leslie Callahan

which was The Subway Bedrace for Bridging, which began in 1999 soon after the tubing hill was open. Crystal Bowersox, an American Idol Runner-up, was the featured celebrity. Crystal was not one to sit around and instead she went snowboarding all day! Bridging was founded on one simple, yet powerful idea— that together we can create a bridge between those in need and those with excess. Since the first donated item, Bridging has provided the basic home essentials to over 90,000 families. J.Marie Fieger of Nemer Fieger PR agency approached Jessica, after rejections from a few other ski areas with the idea of having

mattresses covered in vinyl race down our snow-tubing hill. The race awards participants (in teams of 4) in three catagories: best costumes, most money raised, and the actual race winners. This event stands out due to the creativity of the costumes, the great bands, and the 600 people who are in attendance every year! To date the Subway Bedrace for Bridging has raised over 1 million dollars at Buck Hill!

Tubing became very popular very quickly. Buck Hill was a great venue for parties!

The summer of 1999, Barry Jaeger, an ex Buck Hill racer, and Don McClure took on the racing hill project which they had designed. The improvements involved a re-grading at the top of the hill to facilitate easier use of the rope tow so that the smaller racers could reach the top unaided. It also included a redesign of the 30 foot high starting ramp and the lift operator house. Much of the labor for this project was done by Buck Hill Team members and parents.

Bucky's favorite outdoor activity is tubing.

In late November of 1999, some of Buck Hill's neighbors were evidently having a hard time sleeping due to our snowmaking during the night hours. On December 20th, an emergency Burnsville City Council meeting was held to deal with this problem. After more than an hour of lively testimony – most of it from people on Buck Hill's side – the City Council approved an amendment that affirmed the company's right to make snow between 10 p.m. and 7 a.m. Buck Hill had used the cold-weather overnight hours to make snow, especially in the early season since snowmaking was installed in 1961. The support of Buck Hill employees, patrollers, instructors, and neighbors was overwhelming. This also included the City of Burnsville staff and elected officials. It was truly a heart-warming experience to see one after another, about 30 people in all, tell the city representatives what Buck Hill meant to them. Former mayor Connie Morrison, always a friend of Buck Hill's, came to our defense in this very crucial matter. Don McClure did an outstanding job of presenting our position, which had a very satisfying conclusion.

At the annual shareholders meeting, held December 14, 1999, it was reported that both Powder Ridge and Buck Hill had record breaking 1998-1999 winter seasons. Jerry Wahlin, now in his 14th year as general manager of Powder Ridge reported it was the area's best gross sales year by 8%. He also indicated that season pass sales for the upcoming season had nearly doubled to date. Don McClure, in his 4th season as general manager at Buck Hill, also reported that in spite of the unseasonably warm weather and the late December 7th start to the season, Buck Hill also had an increase in gross sales and season passes.

New Years Eve 1999 and the end of the century brought very sad news to the Buck Hill community. Our Adult Racing Program director, and long time friend, Gabe Cyr, died in an automobile accident near her home. Her dog Jazz, who always traveled with her survived and was fine. It would be impossible for me to relate how much Gabe meant to us at Buck Hill as a friend and as an employee. Gabe received many accolades in the press over the years. In 1970, she was on the cover of *Ski Area Management Magazine*. Highlights of the article included the fact that "Gabrielle Cyr has been directing operations at Pine Bend Ski Area since her husband Oscar died in 1966 and the area's growth is a testimony to her success. Gabe's daughter, Gady Blake, a certified PSIA instructor, helps out in the ski school, headed by Larry Klick and Bob Boyd. Few men could qualify her success with that subtle, 'Not bad, for a woman.' Pine Bend started literally

Gabe in her office with Jazz, her dog, who you can't see.

in her back yard. She and her husband Oscar built a house on a hill overlooking the Mississippi River. One day they decided to install a small rope tow, and soon their friends were skiing with them on weekends. A few years and more friends

106

later, the Cyr's realized they were in business. They bought a sign, purchased more acreage, and in 1953 formed the Ski Pine Bend Co." Can you imagine that happening today? It would take a year just to do the environmental studies and at least a million dollars!

Nancy added, "We have quite an extensive adult racing program and Gabe was in charge of doing the timing, organizing the schedules of adult and high school teams, and that was an important job and she handled it very well." Don McClure, general manager at Buck Hill, commented that, "Her life touched three generations within the skiing community, from people who worked with her to those who skied with her at Pine Bend." Patricia Lecy added "She's such an original, she's not like anyone else I know. She appears rough and tough, but she's got a marshmallow heart." Pine Bend had to cease operations in 1970 because a nearby refinery was polluting the air and causing havoc with the snow. It was a beautiful area situated on the bluffs of the Minnesota River, southeast of the Twin Cities.

We held a memorial service for Gabe at Buck Hill which included her favorite local jazz trio. Buck Hill also holds a memorial ski race every year in her honor at its annual New Year's Eve celebration in conjunction with Friends of the Mississippi River, a charitable organization that cares for the land where Pine Bend Ski Area was located. In December 1993, Gabe received the Ralph Thornton Memorial Award for her contributions to the Twin Cities ski industry. Tammy Coyne who had worked with Gabe for many years continued as director of the amateur racing programs. It required a special skill to coordinate all the different teams and events and Tammy was very adept at the challenge.

All lit up for nighttime fun at Powder Ridge.

2000 - 2010

Record Day, Lexus Tomba Tour, Dash for Cash, Dartmouth Memorial, Wonder Carpet, Triple Chair Lift, Power Ridge Spinoff, U.S. Ski Hall of Fame, Wind Energy, Quad Chair Lift, Zombi Board Shop and Frightmares

A beautiful sunset behind Buck Hill, even though it was -10 degrees outside!

The 2000-2001 season started at Buck Hill with a new record. On Saturday, November 18th (opening day), we had the biggest one-day-sale ever; over 2,000 lift tickets were sold. It seems that at the turn of the century a significant number of unsolicited potential buyers appeared on our doorstep. We spent a considerable amount of time and energy listening to the proposals. The company did not aggressively pursue the sale of Buck Hill at any time. There just seemed to be a flurry of people who came along who thought they might like to own a ski area. We also considered a partnership with the Beaver Mountain Water Slide at that time but to no avail.

Three generations of skiers - Nancy, Jessica, and Madeleine.

Soon after our popular New Year's Eve event, The Lexus Tomba Tour, presented by Rossignol, came to Buck Hill on February 5-6, 2000. After talking with a few other ski areas, Gary Ladd, of Rossignol Ski Company, contacted Jessica and it was agreed she would chair the event. The tour allowed racers to go head-to-head against dynamic, three-time Olympic Gold medalist, Alberto Tomba, aka "The Italian Stallion." This event raised money for children's charities and junior ski racing programs. Buck Hill was the second stop of the tour; other sites that year were Stratton Mountain, Northstar-at-Tahoe, Deer Valley and Beaver Creek. The weekend event brought great media exposure, lots of fun for racers of all ages, including a clinic for kids. We had a huge VIP tent in front of the main chalet complete with a parquet wood floor, pasta bar, autograph signing, and merchandise for sale. On Saturday evening, we had a grand party at the newly opened St. Paul Science Center with appetizers, live music and awards.

Eldon Hugelen was a newcomer to the Buck Hill kitchen staff early in 2000 and took great pride in making those very tasty

Alberto Tomba with enthusiastic young racers, 2000.

and popular donuts. Eldon wrote:

> Donuts were the first job in the kitchen each morning as they were made in the grill area. Since high school students are in school each day, it fell to me to make the donuts. How many years Buck Hill has made donuts, I do not know, but during the years I was there, countless parents brought their children to have a Buck Hill donut that they had enjoyed as a kid. This worked out so Gaylord and his boot camp class would have fresh donuts 3 days a week. Gaylord was always complimentary and I made sure there were 2 chocolate dipped donuts for him.

Eldon also has fond memories of the staff:

Shortly after I started to work at Buck Hill, Sharon Throne became kitchen manager. This began a thirteen year working connection with 'the red head' as she was sometimes known, and also with her friend Audie Schostag. I learned to respect Sharon and her difficult job of hiring kids who could and would work, and keeping perishable food supplied and fresh for cooking with ever changing weather, and keeping her cool when things did not work out. One day when Olympic skier Kristina Koznick visited the hill, she gifted me a T-shirt with www. Koznick on it which I still have.

Jessica, who grew up racing and had done some pro-racing locally, thought it would be fun to have a Head-to-Head dual ski race, like the McDonald's Cup held at Buck Hill in the early 70's. The first few years we used a blow horn, but Jessica really wanted to find some cattle gates to make it official. Eventually, she found a pair used in the 80's Peugeot Pro Ski Tour, at Blackjack in Upper Michigan. It took her two years to talk them into giving them up. Don negotiated a price, and local ski racer, Steve Lindemere, picked them up as he was racing there the following week. The Dual Dash for Cash was a big success, paid out thousands over the years, and left memories forever.

We also added the Daktronics

Digital Display board and it turned out to be a very popular feature for the many race programs. Racers could now see their results instantaneously upon completing their runs. We could also keep our guests updated on upcoming events and other amenities we had to offer at the area. In the past, Chuck used to make these announcements on the loud speaker. I fondly recall him saying after each announcement, "Give it a Whirl!"

Getting the display board up was not easy. Don had to spend quite a bit of time convincing the City of Burnsville that the cars on the freeway would not be distracted by the display. In fact, the display was installed behind the main chalet and the parking lot which had been paved and curbed. New landscaping with fir and spruce trees had been installed on the built up berm along the frontage road between the highway and the parking lot. Mayor Kautz intervened on our behalf which was very helpful. In fact, Mayor Elizabeth Kautz was always very supportive of Buck Hill.

Groundbreaking Buckstone Lodge, 2000

On June 16, we received a formal Preliminary Scope of Work document from Tim Olinger of Miller Architects and Builders for construction of what was to become the Buckstone Lodge. It stated a preliminary budget of $1,130,684 and we soon agreed to terms. Tim and his company were a pleasure to work with on this very exciting project for Buck Hill. Of course there were a "few" additions to that original quote.

In 2000 Chuck's friends started a memorial fund for him to be used at the Dartmouth Ski-Way. This effort was spearheaded by Dave Cost and Fred Carelton. In January of 2001, there was a dedication ceremony for the new McClane Family Lodge. At that time, a plaque with Chuck's name was placed on 3 chairs on the Winslow lift. Our daughters, Jessica Stone and Polly Hanson, and Polly's husband Fridolf, joined me for the event. There was a junior race being held that day and several of the racers were from Buck Hill; one of them was Martina Sailer, Erich and Ursula's daughter. There is a book written by Stephen Waterhouse, *Passion for Skiing*, that encompasses the history of skiing at Dartmouth. It includes a piece about Chuck and Buck Hill which was written by Doug Tengdin, a former Buck Hill racer and Dartmouth graduate.

Buckstone Lodge and Ski School Entrance

At our spring board of directors' meeting in 2000, both areas reported an outstanding past ski season in spite of it being a very short one. In a letter to the shareholders, I reported that: "The book value per share of Buck Hill stock has increased in value in the last 5 years by 74%. This can be attributed to our dedicated and enthusiastic employees at both areas. Congratulations are in order for the Buck Hill Ski Patrol, headed by Dave Krutzig. The ski patrol was the recipient of several prestigious awards this year. Shirley Schoenbauer*, who is seen here almost on a daily basis, won the All Pro National Patroller award." Don reported, "The 1999-2000 was the shortest season on record after 1962, with Buck Hill only operating for 79 days. However, it turned out to be our 5th consecutive record-setting season with sales up 14% over the previous one."

Casey Wahlin at Powder Ridge, 2000.

Meanwhile, Powder Ridge was preparing for the 2000-2001 season. Inside the latest brochure you could see all that was going on at the area. Some programs were new and some tried and back by popular demand. These included the Kids Club, Twelve Buck Nights, Ladies Day, New Years Eve Family Night, Church Night, and the Super Bowl Sunday Special.

In the spring of 2001, The Buck Hill Employee Scholarship program was put in place. It was aimed at helping the many high school and college students who worked at Buck Hill with some of their education expenses. The applicants provided some information and they were recommended by their various department supervisors. Five scholarships were given and the recipients were quite thankful. All Buck Hill employees received a number of other benefits, including a special price for a season pass for anyone in the immediate family. We also gave them 50% off of ski and snowboard rental packages, 30% off ski school lessons and programs such as the Developmental Ski Racing Team (D-Team) and the USSA Ski Team directed by Erich Sailer. Another benefit was 50% off on food in the main chalet.

At the board meeting in April of 2001, Don reported that the skier visits were 146,000 this year compared to 116,000 last season. The good weather contributed to this growth. The tubing operation was up 34% over the previous season. Don and Gregg expressed satisfaction with the progress of the building project and with good cooperation from the builder. Tom Schulz gave a report on the ski school and he thought the new space under the Whittier Room for the ski school will certainly help serve the public in more efficient ways. Gregg presented a financial report and the board members offered compliments to him for quality work in organizing the financial records of the ski areas and submitting them in a timely manner.

In 2001, the Wonder Carpet made in Austria was installed on Teachers Pet. It was a moving walkway, much like those at airports, that takes beginners up the hill. It was great because it did all of the work – no sitting or holding was required, skiers just enjoyed the ride! This lift was very helpful in getting beginners to enjoy skiing because they no longer feared the dreaded rope tow, and they avoided the pileups that often clogged it at various points along the ride.

Excitement reigned on Dec. 3, 2001, when the new Buckstone Lodge was officially dedicated with a grand party in the Whittier Room! It was planned that skiers and snowboarders would be cascading down the slopes that night providing a spectacular view for our guests. However, it had been a very warm fall and the area was not open. Fortunately, it was cold enough to make snow that night so the view was not entirely lost. It was a gala event. Many friends and employees were among the party goers. The Very Reverend Douglas Fontaine gave the invocation and his wife Jeanne attended also. There were employees from the first year of operation which included Joan McCaull Strand, Nancy Wiegand Hirshfield, Donna Thompson Klass, and Diane Robinson. They had all flipped burgers in our primitive kitchen in the fifties. A good time was had by all.

Dedication night of the Buckstone Lodge.
December 3, 2001

Dedication Night - Jessica Stone,
Bucky, and Nancy Stone

At a February 2002 board meeting, Don mentioned that this was the third year the replacement of the Gawn chairlift had been discussed. He explained in very technical terms why he thought this lift must be a first priority. The lifts capacity was no longer sufficient and it required a great deal of annual maintenance, therefore it must be replaced. Don received a bid from Jan Leonard at DOPPELLMAYR-CTEC for a triple chair lift for $324,800. It was approved by the board and installed in time for the 2002-2003 season. I proposed the idea that we develop the Walsh Property with some fun terrain such as bumps and moguls specifically for children with the goal of increasing revenues perhaps by 10%. We might build a bridge over the tubing hill for access to the main area. It could be called The Outbuck, but it was not to be, as we sold the property.

Jessica reported that the restaurant and banquet facility in the new Buckstone Lodge definitely needed some better and more experienced management. There were many inefficiencies and cost lapses. We had very little experience in operating a restaurant and bar. In April, we leased the operations in the lodge to Kramer Catering Co. of Burnsville.

In a letter to the shareholders in November of 2002, I wrote about our overall position.

Wyatt Wiltgen on the brochure cover in 2002-2003

Season pass sales continued to increase as they have in the past six years, in spite of the fact that last season we did not open Buck Hill until December 9th for lack of cold enough weather to make snow. The growth of Buck Hill in the past six years has been quite remarkable. Since 1996, we have built the Buckstone Lodge, with 10,000 sq. ft. of banquet space and a new home for the Chuck Stone Ski and Snowboard School. We have 800 new ski packages and 200 new snowboard packages available for rental. There is also a new handle tow in the mini half pipe area, for the smaller riders.

Just this year we have installed a DOPPELLMAYR - CTEC triple chair

lift and last year the addition of the Wonder Carpet was a very popular lift for beginners. There have also been major improvements to the hill such as a complete re-grading of the beginner's area and we have upgraded and enhanced the snowboard park on the south end of the area. 50 new snow guns have been added, including 40 new high efficiency HKD Tower snow

A man-made blizzard at Buck Hill.

guns and 10 Swedish Areco fan snow guns. Therefore, we are in a much better position to make snow in marginal weather.

An article by Stephanie Pearson in the February 2003 issue of *Ski Magazine* made the point that a tiny Midwestern ski area (Buck Hill), proved that it didn't take thousands of skiable acres to produce Olympic champions:

> Vail, Colorado, and Buck Hill are sister mountains of sorts: Both ski areas were started with help from 10th Mountain Division members, both regularly crank out Olympic-caliber skiers, and both have dramatic views of an interstate. Sure, Vail can boast a few thousand more skiable acres - 5,249 more to be exact. But what Buck Hill lacks in mountain real estate, it makes up for in rope-tow assisted repetition. Where else can competitive skiers run 400 gates on a school night?

This article continues in the racing section of this book.

Max Wiltgen decided to give snowboarding a whirl.

In July of 2003, *Ski Area Management* reported the NSAA's (National Ski Areas Association) unofficial tally of 57.6 million skier/rider visits topped the record of two years ago by a slim 6%. Every US region had near record visits, most significantly in the Midwest, where visits jumped 18% over the previous year.

In a Burnsville City Council work session in 2003, it was announced that its intention was to rezone Buck Hill Ski Area from its current R-1A (rural residential) zoning designation. This would allow a change from single family homes to be developed on the site, to a zoning that would be more consistent with the city's Comprehensive Plan, and also consistent with Buck Hill's plans. Most council members wanted the rezoning to be based on the land use that it was at that time in 2003, which of course was a ski area. At the September 17th board meeting, the directors decided to lay out a Planned Unit Development, with legal advice for submission to the city. The result of these meetings was a new zoning category called commercial

Tarquin Hanson came all the way from Conneticut to ski at Mont Le Buc.

recreation specifically for Buck Hill.

In the summer of 2003, Phil Marick returned to Buck Hill as the new manager of the rental shop. Phil was a great skier and had perfected his skills on the Buck Hill Race Team in the late 80's. He had also worked in the ski school as a ski school supervisor. After some years in Colorado, Phil was back and went to work in the rental department. He redesigned the work space, built tech benches, and reconfigured the space to make the equipment fit better. This was a remarkable achievement considering the lack of space there was to work with! Phil and his crew could push out over 30,000 rental packages a year. In 2010, he became manager of the race department as well with Julie Welsh as his chief assistant. Phil became known as the director of stuff. He always had great insight into the ever changing ski industry.

Phil Marick - Director of Stuff

After several years of preparation, Buck Hill, Inc. announced the spinoff of Powder Ridge in July of 2004. Powder Ridge General Manager, Jerry Wahlin, and Area Outdoor Manager, Layne Anderson, purchased the area from the Buck Hill Corporation. Jerry came to the area in 1984 from Trollhaugen Ski Area. Layne had worked at Powder Ridge for 19 years in many different capacities including outdoor manager. He was born and raised in the Kingston/Litchfield area where he continued to farm during the off season. Both men, having worked at the "The Ridge" for years, felt their business adventure as owners was a continuation of work they love. Although all of us will miss our relationship with "The Ridge," it only made sense for this spinoff to take place and we wished them all the luck and good weather in the world. Jerry Wahlin was confident of the venture as he recalled, "We had no doubt Power Ridge would be successful. We had many wonderful employees. The staff at Powder Ridge has always been the backbone of The Ridge."

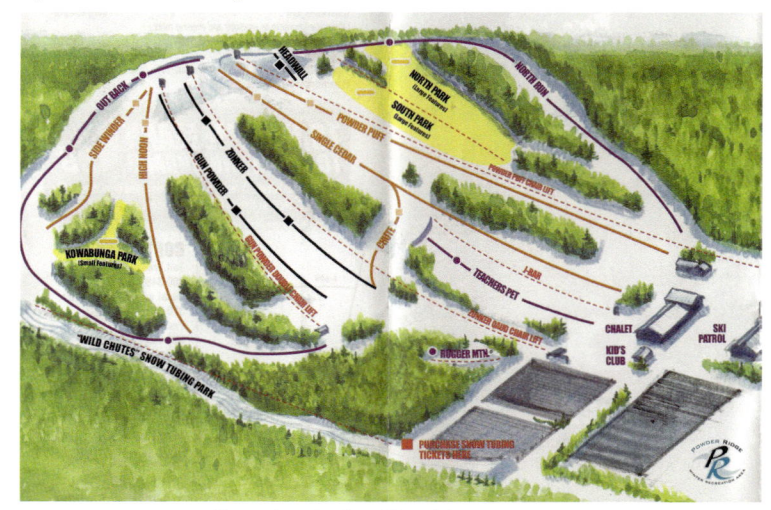

Powder Ridge Trail Map, 2007

Janet Robinson, a key staff member, was working as group sales and office manager even before Jerry arrived. Other key members were Terry Nelson (rental manager), Mary Heid (kitchen manager), Mark Jansky, and Bob Stein. Terry and Mary had been with Powder Ridge for over 30 years, and Mark and Bob had been running the hill operations for many years as well. Jerry and Layne worked with so many good people who genuinely cared about Powder Ridge. Powder Ridge's success was because of these people and they could not have been more pleased knowing that its future was in such good hands.

The spinoff was also the beginning of Buck Hill's enduring relationship with attorney Bill O'Brien, of DeWitt, MacKall, Crounse and Moore.

The summer of 2005 saw some major investments at Buck Hill. We purchased a new Pisten Bully groomer and a Zaugg half pipe groomer manufactured in Switzerland. New high efficiency motors had been installed on the snowmaking pumps. We continued to expand the terrain park with professionally manufactured features from Rail Builder of Lake Tahoe, California. The investment in the terrain park has made it one of the most popular runs at the area.

Meanwhile at Buck Hill, the Callahans were a family affair. Leslie Callahan came to work at Buck Hill in October of 2004, where she had previously learned to snowboard under the excellent tutelage of Dianna Drake. Leslie worked in the ticket office with Gail Stoeber as manager, soon to be followed by Chris Schorn. Leslie became the manager of the ticket office in 2007 and found that the old saying "The customer is always right" was true! Her son, Jason, worked part time in the rental department and daughter, Nickie, worked part time in the cafeteria in the main chalet. Both were students at Lakeview North High School. I once heard Leslie say, "It was the best job I ever had."

Leslie Callahan taking a break from the ticket office on the new airbag.

It was reported to the board members on March 3, 2005: "Our pattern of record breaking winter seasons has come to a screeching halt this year. We are approximately 10% behind last year and we're thankful it is not more as we have heard via the industry that other areas were not so lucky. A very warm November was not conducive to snow-making and we opened on the 13th with only a few runs. Weekends were lost to wind, rain, and below zero weather. If it didn't get as cold as the media said it would, it did not matter, as the media made sure you would not dare venture outside." In April, Don reported that a snowy, cold March enabled the area to salvage the season.

David Tengdin spearheaded a successful quest for Erich Sailer's induction into the U.S. National Ski Hall of Fame. On September 26th, 2005, the inductees were announced and included Hillary Lindh, David (Darcy) Brown, Walter Foeger, and Erich Sailer. Erich was ranked among America's most successful coaches. He earned the nickname of the "Yoda" of ski coaching, training racers year round with race camps at Mt. Hood, Oregon, Winter Park, Colorado, and Hintertux, Austria. At one point in their lives, every skier on the 2002 U.S. Olympic Women's Slalom Team had been under Erich's guidance. His most successful protégés include U.S. Ski Team members Kristina Koznick, Tasha Nelson, Sarah Schleper, Lindsey Kildow (Vonn), Resi Stiegler, and Julia Mancuso. The induction ceremony was held on Friday, April 28, 2006 in Ishpeming, Michigan, recognized as the birthplace of organized skiing in America and home to the U.S. National Ski Hall of Fame and Museum.

Almost 2 year old Campbell Hanson, taking some runs with her dad Fridolf.

In 2005, Don initiated the move to bring wind energy to Buck Hill. Originally, we wanted to put a wind tower on the top of the hill, but the neighbors protested as they thought it would be too noisy so it did not happen. Dakota Electric Association's newsletter in the spring of 2005 reported that Buck Hill Ski Area, in a commitment to renewable energy sources, recently agreed to purchase more than one million kilowatts of Wellspring Renewable Wind Energy annually. This volunteer purchase from Dakota County Electric Association meant that all of Buck Hill's energy was generated by wind. Purchasing this large amount of wind energy annually was the equivalent of planting more than 200 acres of trees.

Buck Hill Ski Area was proud to support Dakota Electric's Wellspring program. It was in the business of healthy,

Some Stone Family Skiers - Top: Polly Hanson, Max Wiltgen, Emily Stone, Jenny Stone, Madeline Wiltgen, Nancy Stone. Bottom: Tarquin Hanson, Wyatt Wiltgen, Charlie Hanson, Campbell Hanson, Jessica Wiltgen

Familiar faces: Jac Papineau, Chris Heid, Dawn Cronsdale, Phil Marick, Chris Schorn, Tammy Coyne, Don McClure, Tom Schulz, Gregg Eppich, Brad Scanlon, Jason Schulberg

outdoor living, so what better way to emphasize that than by helping our environment? In keeping with its desire to be environmentally friendly, Buck Hill also updated its ski lifts with energy-efficient motors and drives. At the National Ski Area Association's annual meeting that year, Buck Hill received the Silver Eagle Award for energy conservation.

In the spring of 2006, we were looking for a new partner for the Buckstone Lodge food service. With its convenient location in Lakeville, Crystal Lake Golf Club became our new food service provider that year and lasted until 2015. It made a lot of sense with opposite seasons. Those people in charge of operations were manager Lorie Kjergaard, Diane Sprauge who aptly handled catering, banquets and group sales and she was assisted by Victoria Kelliher. I enjoyed knowing a lot of the waitress's and one who always made me feel very special was Frances DeBaun. I usually ordered the Buck Burger, with fries of course.

On September 12, 2006, in a letter to the shareholders, they were informed that the past 18 months had been very busy ones. Quite a bit of time was spent working out the details of our land sale to Plowshares. It comprised of the undeveloped Walsh property adjacent to Buck Hill on the north. The sale was completed and there was an offering from Buck Hill, Inc. to the shareholders, if they wanted to sell their stock at this time. One of the conditions of the sale was that the City of Burnsville would only issue development rights to Plowshares if Buck Hill remained a recreational facility with a ski hill and related activities. That of course, had always been our intention. There was a good response to the shareholders buy-back offer. Twenty-one shareholders, representing 80,000 shares of stock had been tendered to

121

Original Mouse Pass Sign on the frontage road.

Jessica Stone and Brooks Chandler at the relocated Mouse Pass

the corporation.

The 2006-2007 Buck Hill Brochure announced: "Welcome to Buck Hill's 53rd winter season of family fun. We have a great year ahead with many improvements and achievements over the past year. During the summer, Buck Hill installed a new quad chair lift to service the south end of the hill. This chair replaces the Miner Denver and the Hall Chair lifts that serviced some of our beginner terrain and snowboard park. When we installed the new lift, we added 125,000 cubic yds. of fill to the top of the hill to make our snowboard park bigger and better than ever."

Chuck's favorite, Mouse Pass, originally on the frontage road, was relocated this year to connect the top of the Doppelmayr Quad with a new trail called Mouse Pass that went behind the old Quad and took you over to the north side of the area. This was a much more convenient way to get to the north side and the Buckstone Lodge from the new Quad, rather than going up and down and up and down again. It reminded me of catwalks out west, but just a touch shorter.

Tom Warner resigned from the board in 2006, after 50 years of service. It would be impossible to describe the positive contribution that Tom had made to the success of the company. We held a surprise Thank You Party for Tom that was attended by his wife, Barbara, and many members of their family, as well as a good number of board members. Tom was very surprised and a good time was had by all.

Barbara and Tom Warner at his surprise party.

Ski Magazine, February 2007, had an article by Joe Cutts on Buck Hill and it was mostly about racing (see racing section). However, Joe did capture a bit about the Stone's winter life in the 60's and 70's:

In the winter, Buck

became the Stone family room. Stoney the dog, born under a brush pile at the hill, ran up the slopes under the lifts, then chased the children back down the hill. Nancy's daughter, Jessica, remembers marching into the kitchen to prepare grilled cheese sandwiches the way she liked them. And Buck thrived during the skiing

Don grooming with the new Pisten Bully.

glamour years in the 60's and 70's. Each spring when the hill closed, the Stone family piled into the car for a skiing trip out west and there was usually a ski race involved for one of the girls. Jessica remembers that the first stop at each ski area was the maintenance shop where her dad would compare lift technology with the local workers. We always had to go look at the bull wheels.

In April 2007, to maintain first class snow making, Don proposed a five-year snowmaking project, with a $60,000 investment each year. All pipes would be replaced at the conclusion of the program. He said we also needed soil stabilization at the top of the new hill. He further reported that the area was fully green - all power at the area originated from wind power purchased by the ski area. Buck Hill was ahead of its time in its energy conservation.

Colorful young boarders and Don in his office.

Late in 2007, I wrote to the shareholders about the very busy and productive summer season: "The Buck Hill Ski Team's club room has been completely remodeled. This project includes a large drop off area, new staircase, landscaping and a lighted sign that features the teams' logo and Erich Sailer 2005 Ski Hall of Fame recipient. The number of junior racers has grown significantly in the past few years. This was a record year for the team in terms of growth. Other improvements included an addition to the deck on the main chalet and upgrades for race city."

The Buck Hill Ski Patrol continued to be among the best in the United States. In 2007, a handful of patrollers received some very significant awards including

Erich and Nancy at Winter Park 2011

Regional Alpine Patrol of the Year. Kerstin Hammarberg, our current patrol director, received the Western Region and Central Division Alpine Patroller of the Year award.

In April of 2008, Buck Hill was mentioned in an article from *The New York Times*. We were thrilled that we had been noticed, and it primarily commented about the success of one of Buck Hill's racers, Lindsey Kildow Vonn. That year Lindsey became the first American Woman since 1983 to win the World Cup Championship. It also made note that our racing club received two prestigious awards - the USSA Club of the Year award and the 2008 Alpine Club of the Year award. It went on to say how strong the racing program had become under Erich Sailer's leadership and commended its consistency of its junior racers. Credit was given to Erich's system of hiring team alumni and former World Cup athletes, which brought that winning perspective to the junior racers. The world cup racers could illustrate just how winning was done.

Also in April at the board meeting, Don reported that it had been a good year in spite of the fact there had been no natural snow in January and February. Gregg Eppich gave a very detailed financial report that showed excellent growth at the area. Due to the strong financial position of the company, the board approved a dividend for the shareholders of $1.00 per share. A

Miss Campbell Hanson came to try the Magic Carpet

A cozy ride in a Minnesnowta winter.

Construction of the new Magic Carpet

Might be four times the capacity of a rope tow.

new conveyor lift, an 800 ft. Magic Carpet will be installed this summer and at that time, it was the longest one in North America. We also purchased a new 2009 Kassbohrer PB 400 Park Bully for grooming, replacing an older groomer which was traded in on the new one. A thorough discussion was given to the possibility of doing a Haunted House Halloween event at Buck Hill.

On the national scene, the news was very good for the 2007-2008 ski/snowboard season business. Skier/snowboard visits topped 60.1 million which was a 9.1% increase from the 55.1 million visits recorded in the 2006-2007 season. This increase included a 12.3% rise in the Midwest region, all very good indicators for the ski business.

It was a lucky day for Buck Hill when Shawn Solem decided to move his Zombi Boardshop to its present location in 2008, just down the road from us. He was instrumental in promoting a lot of fun events for the snowboarders. A very popular event with 50 or 60 kids age 12 and under was held several Saturdays during the season with awards for beginners, intermediates and advanced Little Jibbers. There were very nice medals and prizes awarded at the event. Early in the season, the Boardshop held The Shred til You're Dead snowboarding event with cash prizes and free Shred T-shirts for the first 50 to register. This was followed at the end of the season by The Last Slash. There was pond skipping, snowboarding, music, prizes and good vibes. Both events were very popular with the snowboarding crowd. There were also the Thursday Night Throw Downs for all ages with Rails, Big Air, and Halfpipe at different events and trophies too.

Pat Milbery brought his So-Gar Snowboard Camp Tour to Buck Hill and it was also a popular event at which snowboarders learned a lot, had a good time and went home with lots of great prizes.

We were fortunate to have Chris

Beautiful snow for the future halfpipe.

Rachel and her dad Chris in 2009. She just qualified for the State High School meet.

Omodt* in the security department since 1998. Chris did scheduling and other important tasks that happened to arise. His expertise and dependability, as well as the other security officers, made a huge difference in staving off potential theft and behavior problems.

In September of 2009, we entered the Haunted Halloween world with our own scary version and called it Frightmares at Buck Hill. Don and several other employees had gone to some Halloween shows that were held every year to promote the industry. There were always new monsters and other paraphernalia to scare the wits out of the terror seekers. We consulted with a well known guru in the industry and he was very sure that we could be quite profitable with a haunt at Buck Hill and so were we. We also visited the local Halloween attractions and thought we could do as well if not better. We were excited about the possibilities of having a profitable operation to offset the ski season.

Emily Stone taking some runs with Bucky, aka her dad.

Charlie Hanson snowboarding at Mont Le Buc.

2010 - 2015

*More Frightmares, Rise of Social Media,
Gold Medal, Recession, Current Employees,
Board of Directors, Vail, Sale of Buck Hill*

My creative cousin Jonathan Horton, an accomplished artist with experience in the movie industry, came from California to design the sets and costumes. Jonathan had first done some work for Buck Hill in 1982 just after he had graduated from the California College of Arts. He refinished tables in The Bucket and constructed some abominable snow monsters for the kiddies to ski around and about during ski school lessons.

Jonathan wrote:

Cousins, Jonathan Horton and Nancy - Do you see the family resemblence?

I found Chuck to be an extremely positive individual, his enthusiasm was contagious and inspiring. He discussed at that time doing a haunted hayride project for the fall season. It didn't happen that season, but it did come up regularly for the next decade. Meanwhile I had returned to California and began working in the film industry. The idea of a haunt came back as a definite project in 2009 and I was hired by Don McClure to work on it. That summer the main chalet became a paint studio.

For several weeks, scenic flats were decorated with a variety of faux finishes. Plywood panels were transformed into Victorian lathe and plaster walls covered with decaying moldy wallpaper and ancient wainscoting, "stone crypts," and glow in the dark hallucinations of the insane. Later they were carried to the hillside to be assembled into a haunted asylum, a vampire-infested manor house and a cursed, paint factory. During that summer of creating Frightmares at Buck Hill, I often thought of Chuck Stone and the opportunity he had given me all of those years ago, and wished he could have seen what we had accomplished.

As fun as it was building Frightmares, it was even better to play/act in it. The first season I became a vampire, making the guests - girls, boys, and grown-ups alike squeal in terror. There were a lot of cold nights that first year and snow arrived in September. A glass of whisky in the Bucket at the end of the night was often a pleasant way to end the evening.

The following year was also very cold. I tramped up and down the hill costumed as a horned devil, moving fast to keep warm. In 2012, I was determined to be better prepared for the bracing Minnesota outdoors.

I created a head-to-toe fur costume of long-haired wool. I prowled the magic carpet as a shaggy, horned demon walking many miles in a night without going anywhere. Unfortunately, that year it was quite warm and I had rather a soggy costume at the end of each evening. Curiously, it wasn't until early 2013 when I visited to go over plans for the next and last season of Frightmares, that I first saw Buck Hill in its winter mode, covered with snow and full of skiers.

Joy Peterson, of the *Minneapolis Star and Tribune*, wrote an article in 2010, about Frightmares:

An eerie mood has overtaken the slopes at Buck Hill in Burnsville, transforming the black-diamond runs into haunted hills for the Halloween season. And in it's second year, Frightmares gained momentum. Nearly 1,500 people per weekend, passed through its four eerie attractions in the opening weekends in October.

As participants move on, a new 3D experience is found in the Fright Factory. Through stories of the haunted hills, participants can experience different sensory scares in four venues. The story begins in the Orchard Manor, the typical, haunted house of the Frightmares' attractions. The dream for a Scottish immigrant, Hector Cromarty, and his young bride, Mary, was a beautiful Victorian home in the rolling hills. Soon after they moved in, Mary died and Hector went insane, attributed to the evil in the hills. Eventually, a vampire family moved into the home. But the township fought to eliminate them from the area. Now the home is said to be vampire-free and on the market for a new homeowner.

The Horrified Hansons!

McClure said to take note of the mind-bending vortex tunnel, seen through 3D glasses. The Bellharm Lovejoy Asylum is a pitch black experience, complete with a claustrophobic squeeze through a padded room, which patrons need to navigate to get out of the insanity.

Bridging the slopes with the frights, the Haunted Hollow uses a "magic carpet" to bring patrons to the top of a hill for a stroll of screams

130

through the woods on the grounds. McClure recommends good walking attire.

But, wouldn't you know – the first year of Frightmares was the state's coldest October in history. We also received 7 inches of rain and 4 inches of snow. Despite the weather, we had great press coverage and some very good reviews from many patrons who went through the different attractions. Tom Schulz was the overseer and he did an extraordinary job of fitting it all together.

Frightmares did see some growth the second year. The feedback continued to be very positive and we were optimistic about its future as ticket sales increased 29% and gross income rose 40% over the previous season. However, at the directors' meeting, after the third year of Frightmares, I reported that the Halloween project, was not the financial success we had anticipated. We all agreed that labor and maintenance costs must be further reduced in order to become profitable.

Hector and his ghost wife, Mary.

Orchard Manor Dead and Breakfast

Watch out for the Shaggy Horned Demon!

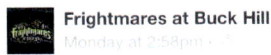

The Asylum Fire.

In October of 2012, the Bellharm-Lovejoy Asylum burned to the ground early one Sunday morning. Our web sight told the sad news and it proved to be a case of arson. Frightmares continued two more years, however as it turned out, it was not a good idea to have another venture that relied on the weather. At the November 2014 board meeting the directors voted to end the event or in other words, "To give up the ghost."

Frightmares at Buck Hill
Monday at 2:58pm ·

The rumors are true. The Bellharm-Lovejoy Asylum burned to the ground early Sunday morning.

The Frightmares at Buck Hill haunt season will begin as planned on October 5th, 2012 with the Haunted Hollow, Orchard Manor Dead & Breakfast, the Fright Factory, and amazing new acts from magician Kevin Hall. Plans are underway to open a new haunt on the former asylum property. We will be posting more details soon!

Although no one was injured in the fire, the residents of the asylum have been displaced and are roaming the area. If you dare to join us for a night of fright this October, we advise you to stay alert. The residents of the former asylum will be lurking in the shadows and they are very unhappy... and hungry.

February of 2010 was a very exciting time for Buck Hill. The Winter Olympics took place in Vancouver, Canada and Buck Hill had one of its own gold medalist contenders, Lindsey Vonn, competing. Buck Hill hosted a viewing party to cheer her on to her gold medal in the downhill. The first ever for an American woman! She also took home a bronze in the super giant slalom event. It is fun to note that our daughter Polly was one of Lindsey's coaches when she was very young.

In the spring, I reported that, "The 2009-2010 winter season, in spite of a struggling economy, the late start/early close and less than ideal weather, the season turned out well. We have a superb staff and dedicated employees and that makes all the difference in any business. The New Years Eve celebration was the busiest day and night of the year."

In the fall of 2010, Julie Welsh took on the task of directing the race department under the guidance of Phil Marick, which included all racing at Buck Hill, other than the USSA racing team. Julie had started her career at Buck Hill in 1986 as a ski instructor under Bobbi Sipe and spent many hours learning and

New Years Eve 2012, L to R: Eldon Hugelen, Sharon Throne, Audie Schostag, and Lynn Anderson

relearning different techniques. She later realized how important it was to have those skills repeated again and again. Julie worked with Tom Schulz for many years in the Ski Wee Program and then managing the FAAST Kids program as it was known. In 2004 she had joined Phil Marick as his assistant in the rental department. Julie said "After we redesigned and set up the area, I learned how to tech skis and how to assemble a snowboard setup with lightning speed. I set up our inventory manuals and kept track of the necessary testing of ski bindings and any equipment that didn't pass inspection." All very important skills to keep Buck Hill running smoothly.

At a November meeting in 2010, Don emphasized how important snow-making is in the ski business. "Last fall, when the weather finally turned cold, we converted 30 million gallons of water into snow in just 12 days." He reported there had been a major flood event that inundated the ski area on August 13th. We received five and a half inches of rain in approximately 45 minutes. The flooding was mainly around the maintenance shop, and we saw all the pumps and motors underwater. It was an expensive and time consuming clean-up, even with the insurance. I brought up my idea of perhaps having a yurt in the woods for the little kiddos in the ski school. I had seen one at the top of Beaver Creek that was very popular. However, when Don approached the city, they said, "No can do," as they could not get the fire trucks up there in the winter. Unbelievable. If a business like Buck Hill were to begin today, with all of the regulations and red tape, it could never happen without millions of dollars. Compare that to our start-up with $3,700!

Marketing Director, Jessica Stone reported that most of the major contracts and media buys were already in place for the coming season. Plans included adding more free events for our guests, digital and stationary billboards, radio, and new TV commercials. Also noted was the rise in social media and all the possibility there for a lower cost.

Mickey Armstrong, Jessica Stone, and Judy Alm - all loyal Buck Hill fans.

The struggle with competition of government owned ski areas continued. In January of 2011, Hennepin County decided to spend $15 million of taxpayer money to make substantial improvements to Hyland Hills Ski area (owned by Hennepin County). The total came closer to $25 million! (Yes, this was our nearest competitor and we had to help finance it.) The Three Rivers Superintendent said, "The chalet built in 1975 is cramped, especially around crowded weekends and holidays..." It was a constant struggle for Buck Hill, and still is, to compete with the government. However, we continued to find enough private funding to make improvements in the free enterprise fashion.

In a letter to the shareholders in the fall of 2011, Don and I reported that Buck Hill's revenues were up for the 2010-2011 season in part due to record snowfall, even though the recession continued to dominate the economic situation in the country. In fact, our financial position was such that we were able to declare a shareholder dividend in May of $1.00 per share.

The year's improvements included repainting all of the buildings and adding new roofs. The lift towers and all the chairs had also been repainted. The snowmaking pipelines were replaced on Milk Run and an Areco snow-making tower was added to Teacher's Pet. The tubing hill had been re-graded and extensive inspection and maintenance was done on all the lifts.

The winter season of 2011-2012 was "the winter that wasn't" according to *Ski Area Management Magazine*. The lack of snow resulted in a lot fewer skiers and snowboarders and severely reduced revenues at most ski areas across the country. That was particularly true of beginners at Buck Hill. We were fortunate that our gross sales were only down 8% from the previous season, which had been a record breaking snowfall year. Many areas in the country saw a 30% decline or more in revenues.

At the 2012 spring board meeting, Don presented a plan for upgrading the snow making system and explained why it was so important. We currently pumped about 2,000 gallons per minute through our system and that volume was a bit more than the recommended capacity. To alleviate the problem, Don proposed that we enlarge the water main from the city water supply, from an 8" pipe to a 12" pipe. We would then be able to pump 7,000 gallons per minute. It would allow Buck Hill to open sooner in the season, which was critical in the late fall. Other capital projects for the off season included the purchase of 4 Areco towers, 1 Techno-Alpine Tower, a Wonder Carpet lift for the tubing hill, additional rentals (skis, boots, boards and bindings), and new ski school uniforms for a grand total of one million dollars.

Rental shop buddies Scott Melby and Willy Williamson

Over the years there have been so many dedicated employees and it has been my intent to mention as many as I could possibly recall for this history. A letter I wrote to the Board of Directors in April 2012, pays homage to some of our current employees, so I am reprinting it here:

At the last board meeting, although we did analyze the numbers and thoroughly discussed our future plans, we did not get to the heart of what makes Buck Hill the success that it is today...its employees. The number after the name is the amount of years he or she has been at Buck Hill.

First of all, we are fortunate to have Don McClure (37) who performs so well as our general manager. He has an expert eye when it comes to mechanical issues and safety. Don is always looking for ways to improve Buck Hill whether it is an air bag, snowmaking, or just some fresh paint. Greg Eppich (15), our very competent controller, knows where every penny is coming from and where it it going. He is adept at financial reports and keeping the company's books in first class order. Jessica Stone (18), our marketing director, does an outstanding job at managing the ever-changing media buys and marketing Frightmares at Buck Hill. Jessica also oversees special party events and in-house events that are designed to engage the skiers and snowboarders. Dave

Holm (21) is a very important contributor to our graphics and website design and maintenance. He supervises the cash room as well.

The outside crew has the unending tasks of lift and vehicle maintenance, snowmaking, snow grooming, and generally keeping the slopes safe for our customers. These hardworking men are Jason Schulberg (20), Jac Papineau (10), Jake Herbeck (10), Britton Lawson (7), Mark Hemeon (5), and Luke Wright (4). We receive many compliments from our skiing and snowboarding customers on our excellent snow conditions, nice lift operators and well groomed runs.

We are also fortunate to have Tom Schulz (17) as Ski School Director. Tom has shown his ability to oversee a very well run ski school, turning children and adults into lifetime skiers and boarders. He has an exceptionally well-trained staff that provides a positive experience for all our customers who come to Buck Hill to learn to ski or snowboard.

Without a doubt, Erich Sailer (43) is the most successful Developmental Junior Ski Racing Coach in the United States. Erich is the recipient of many national awards and has given Buck Hill a world-class reputation of being where great ski racers are born. He is assisted by many fine coaches including Tasha (Nelson) McCrank, a former Olympic racer.

Phil Marick (7) and Julie Welsh (26) do an excellent job of managing the rental department and our very extensive racing programs. These include, but aren't limited to, high school training and races, Ski Challenge, NASTAR, racing clinics, and the never ending phone calls. There is a racing event almost every day of the week and participants range in age from 4 to 84. Gaylord Gladwin (15) conducts adult racing clinics throughout the season. He has a devoted following, especially among the Ski Challenge racers, who take their times quite seriously.

Sharon Throne (10) and Mabeth Dorman (2) manage the Main Chalet Kitchen and are extremely skilled, not only with the food, but with the kids as well. It would take a lot of words to describe the daily happenings that they deal with so patiently.

Charles Stone (18) works in the accounting department. He has set up our in-house video system and sees that it is up to date. He is also a cash manager and helps out in the ticket office and kitchen when extra service is needed.

Leslie Callahan (7) is Buck Hill's ticket office supervisor. She does an outstanding job of keeping the cash registers ringing and answering our guest's questions. I think she knows all the season pass holders by name and there are over 3,000 of them.

Tracy Hemeon (5) is an expert at group sales. It takes a lot of finessing to get the different groups in the right place at the right time and making sure everyone is happy. I have also seen Tracy helping out in other departments at peak times, which is always appreciated.

In the Rental Department, we have Scott Melby (7) and Willy Williamson (7). They do a great job of getting the customers on the slopes in a timely and efficient manner and with a smile. There is also a lot of equipment maintenance. Among many other rental employees are Allie Kastner (8) and Erik Moe (2), whose dependability and friendly customer encounters can always be counted on. Justin Linde started as a ski and snowboard tech and quickly became a night supervisor and the following year became parking lot manager as well.

Dave Chlebeck (3) is the supervisor of the tubing hill, as well as our pro patroller. There are times when there are many people anxious to go tubing which does present a challenge. Dave has a calming effect on the waiting crowd. As a dedicated ski patroller, safety is always high priority with him. Dave has also had his hand in many projects around the hill.

When it comes to Halloween, Geno Peterson (30) is in charge of putting all the haunts together. He also lends his carpentry skills to many of the projects that we always seem to have, including fixing something or making something new. For instance, this summer it will be a covered bridge over the new magic carpet on the tubing hill. Geno is also a cash guy. That's what we call them.

We are fortunate to have one of the best, if not the best, ski patrol in the Midwest. Our Ski Patrol Director is Kerstin Hammarberg (23) and she sees that the patrollers always safely cover the hill, are trained properly and up to date on accreditations. Every patroller contributes to our excellent safety record at Buck Hill.

There are many other employees, too numerous to mention. In the winter alone we have over 350 on the payroll. Needless to say, Buck Hill could not function without them as well.

The Board of Directors has also been a significant factor for the success of Buck Hill in dealing with its "ups and downs." The current members of the board are Jerry Bremer, Stuart Campbell, Greg Eppich, Bruce Freeman, Dick Howell, Colby Lund, Charles McCarthy, Don McClure, Jessica Stone, Dick Strand, Bob Tengdin, and Dave Tengdin. This represents a total of over 360 years of service, including me. Thank you, one and all from the bottom of my heart and have a great summer!

In June of 2012, we were approached by the Vail Corporation. They were on a quest to buy a ski area in the Twin City area, to help promote their many resorts in the west. It was interesting to meet with them and they eventually did buy Afton Alps. Thankfully, the venture did not have a major competitive impact on any of the ski areas, which in the beginning, was a concern for all of us. I guess we thought they might bring one of their mountains out here!

Also in the summer of 2012, Stuart Campbell was presented with a Lifetime Achievement Award at the annual Midwest Ski Area's Association meeting. Stuart began his career at the beginning of Buck Hill in 1954. In 1976, Stuart formed Track Inc., a supplier of ski area equipment. He has served as President of both the Midwest and Central Ski Area Associations, as well as on the board of the National Ski Area Assocation for 7 years. Stuart's achievements in the ski industry have been truly remarkable.

Stuart Campbell - many honors from the ski industry

The 2012-2013 brochure had a lot of news to crow about for the coming season, including a Wonder Carpet servicing the snow tubing park, replacing a handle tow. It made getting up the hill much easier and it has a rustic covered

Margit* and Wilfred Gerhart - loyal Buck Hill skiers for over 30 years!

More loyal skiers - Bob Manuel, Stan (Stosh) Novak, and Wilfred Gerhart.

canopy. A 50-foot airbag was installed for kids and adults who wanted to perfect their aerial skills. The rental shop has 600 pairs of new skis and bindings and we also purchased all new junior ski boots. The first phase of a three-year upgrade to our snow making system has greatly increased overall capacity.

The 2012-2013 winter season had an unusual amount of cold weekends. The media continued to play up the cold weather which hurt the ski business a lot. People want perfect days and on those days the crowds were large. However, March weather cooperated with the ski areas and we were open until April 5, 2013.

In the October 2013 letter to the shareholders, Don and I compared Buck Hill in 1954 to Buck Hill in 2013: "In 1954 we had about 20 part-time employees who worked on weekends when there was snow. A lot of them worked for $2.00 an hour or free skiing. In 2013, we have ten full time employees who receive full employee benefits and approximately four hundred part-time employees, who also received many benefits including free skiing and snowboarding. We are very fortunate to have such a dedicated staff of employees. In the time period from 2003-2013 we have invested over 10 million dollars in the hill and we had a stock buy back for 3.3 million dollars. These investments made a tremendous difference as they allowed us to be current and remain competitive in this capital intensive business."

Nancy and the Outside Crew: Mike Sisko, Jason Schulberg, Brandon Keiffer, Dave Chlebeck, and Jac Papineau. Summer, 2013.

In May of 2014, Buck Hill Ski Racing Club was awarded a Gold Certificate by the USSA. The Gold-certified clubs are called "The Best in the World." These clubs serve as a model both organizationally and athletically and are resources for the sport as a whole. In the U.S., Gold clubs to date include Buck Hill, Burke Mountain Academy, Steamboat Springs, Winter Park, Vail, Mammoth Mountain, Sun Valley, and Stratton Mountain. Buck Hill is the only area in the Midwest to achieve this status.

The November 2014 board meeting pointed out that the 2013-2014 season was very disappointing, but we did much better than many of the outlying areas. It was an extremely cold winter and the hill closed a record number of days due to the frigid weather. By January 28, schools had been closed five times. The previous season had also been very cold. Don reported that, because of our excellent safety record, Buck Hill was the only local private ski area that remained in the private liability insurance market. The other ski areas were assigned to a risk pool. Our ability to use private liability insurance translated into a savings of approximately sixty thousand dollars per year for Buck Hill. Don went on to explain that Buck Hill's splendid safety record was due in large part to the excellent training and commitment of the Buck Hill Ski Patrol. He also noted that Becky Cromley is the new kitchen manager. Don mentioned that we had another unsolicited inquiry into the possibility of acquiring Buck Hill, Inc. He stressed the need for confidentiality from the board.

Buck Hill's 60th Anniversary was celebrated February 21, 2015 in the Buckstone Lodge and all were invited for food, dancing and live music by the Casablanca Orchestra. The event was well attended and there was a lot of dancing as the music was great. A highlight of the evening was Alan Kildow singing, Sweet Georgia Brown.

Newlyweds Matt and Jenny (Stone) Benusa.

The main purpose of the February 26, 2015 Board meeting was to hear a presentation by David Solner as a potential buyer of Buck Hill. Jerry Bremer explained the various forms of a sale. David came to the meeting with John Cunningham and made his presentation. He said he came from a competitive background in skiing, having been a ski jumper. His vision for Buck Hill was to make it a year round athletic training center, and to put a plastic application on two runs for skiing and snowboarding. This would allow summer skiing and it would be possible to set gates for training purposes. In the future, he wanted to install a 1,200 parking space ramp, expand or replace the existing base facilities, install a gondola, an outdoor amphitheater, a top of the hill facility and an 80 room hotel. He estimated that the listed improvements would take about 3-4

Nancy in 2015 and Nancy in 1954

years to install and cost the neighborhood about $35-40 million dollars.

After David and John left, we discussed the other offers that had been proposed for the purchase of the area and decided to continue negotiations with them all. We continued our analysis with the other offers and reached a final decision. A good omen for the future was the fact that revenues for this past season rose ten percent, a good indication for further growth.

THE SALE OF BUCK HILL. The announcement for the October 15, 2015 Board of Directors meeting read: "The main purpose of this meeting is to approve the Stock Redemption Agreement and the sale of Buck Hill. This will presumably be our last board meeting. Don McClure and Dave Solner will be equal partners in Buck Hill. They have indicated that every board member will receive a lifetime season pass. The vote was unanimous for accepting their offer and putting the future of Buck Hill in their hands."

Don and Malcolm

I was confident that Don McClure and the Solners were the ones to accomplish that task. Don came to the partnership with forty years of experience and expertise in the ski business having done it all. Dave had a very successful career with the Cuningham Group as an architect. He started skiing at the age of 3 and turned to competitive jumping at the age of 7. In the early 80's, while just entering high school,

Dave, Cole, Stone, and Chip Solner.

he was named to the U.S. Ski Jumping Team. Dave's accomplishments in ski jumping included Central Division Class A Champion. He also competed at the international level including a few World Cup events in the U.S. and Europe. Dave is married to Corrine "Chip" Solner and they have two boys, Stone (15) and Cole (13).

Last but not least, the members of the board of directors of Buck Hill have been invaluable to the success of the company. They have earned a special mention and thank-you.

Don Ankeny	Bill McCarthy	Dick Strand
Jerry Bremer	Charles McCarthy	David Tengdin
Walter Bush	Katherine McCarthy	Robert Tengdin
Stuart Campbell	Don McClure	Bruce Thompson
Greg Eppich	Henry Reget	Jerry Wahlin
Bruce Freeman	Glen Stanley	Tom Warner
Harrison Freeman	Chuck Stone	Fred Wells
Dick Howell	Jessica Stone	Pete Wittig*
Colby Lund	Nancy Stone	

Dave Solner's vision for the future of Buck Hill.

Dave Solner designed this sign for the next Buck Hill chapter.

The very first Ski School sign.

Chuck Stone Ski & Snowboard School

Dedicated to the memory of Chuck Stone in December, 2001.

1954-1969

A history of Buck Hill cannot be complete without considerable attention given to the history of its ski school. Just as Buck Hill has evolved, so has its ski school. From its humble beginnings in 1954 to the modern day Chuck Stone Ski and Snowboard School, its mission of teaching the sport to ensure life

Brandy and the 1966 ski school instructors.

long skiers has never changed. I would like to acknowledge Tom Hayden, who wrote this history assisted by Tom Schulz. I have added a bit and shortened it just a touch.

Tom Hayden, showing his enthusiasm for teaching the sport.

The first person to oversee the direction of the ski school was Glen Stanley in 1954. Glen had many years of teaching experience in Minnesota and Sun Valley. He was known for teaching skiers to enjoy the sport immediately. The lack of snow in the early seasons made for an abbreviated version of today's standard of ski school. As the weather cooperated, and the sport of skiing grew in popularity, the ski school numbers also increased. It soon became a necessity to hire a permanent ski school director. Duncan Grandin was the ski school director for the 61-62 season and he was also in charge of the rental department. Stuart (Boot) Gordon was program director. Alex C. Petri opened the season of 62-63 as the first professional director of the Buck Hill ski school. Petri was trained in California and at Big Bromley in Vermont, and thus brought a comprehensive breadth of skiing knowledge. Dave Grofscik was head instructor for several years and was very popular with the students. Night skiing was available and so were ski school lessons.

Early on, racing was popular in the ski school. In 1966, Walter Huestis, Marty Hustad, and Buzz

Duncan Grandin, ski school director in the early 60's.

144

Bainbridge were the first to formally coach a team of twelve boys. Next came Austrian world champion, Tony Spiss, who led instruction the following two years. Later, Gordy Anderson guided the school. By then, the best young racers trained during the summer at the International Summer Racing Camp, owned by Erich Sailer, Pepi Gramshammer, and Andrel Molterer, in Red Lodge, Montana. While at camp in 1969, Cindy Stone (daughter of Chuck and Nancy Stone) became aware that Erich was looking for a coaching job and Cindy knew Buck Hill was looking for a coach.

1969-1980

In the fall of 1969, Erich began as co-director with Gordie Anderson of the ski school at Buck Hill, and just one year later, Erich alone held the reins. In the 1970-1971 season, Fred Adam was the chief instructor. The program flourished under Erich's leadership. Many more Austrians were hired including Horst Falger, Georg Neubauer, and Pepi Pittl. Their colorful personalities were a treat to the young students and racers. Aiding the professional instructors were a group of talented, local, part-time instructors. The Ski School Racing program exploded and there was a need for more leadership in the Ski School.

Austrian Instructors - Reinhart Pedross, Horst Falger, and Pepi Pittl in the 1970's.

An adult ski class in the mid 1970's.

Erich and Ursula, 1978

Erich's wife, Ursula, was a physical education major in Germany and was a perfect fit for filling the role for new assignments at Buck Hill. During the first several years, she coordinated the office and eventually took over the non-racing segment of the ski school. Ursula was a phenomenal skier as well as organized, responsive, and excellent at dealing with many different personalities. Both Erich and Ursula were very particular concerning the people they hired. Every candidate had to pass a skill test in order to become an instructor. Ursula retired when their daughter, Martina, was born in 1980.

1980-1986

Ursula was replaced by Eric Bloomquist, a quietly intense and competitive man. He tried to match his instructions with the students' abilities. He ended each season with a "board meeting" (which was a ski race in which he always managed to win). He led a disciplined staff and never cancelled classes due to the cold. Some of his staff included, Gary Groven, Mike Gove, Bruce Abbe, Davey Nelson, and Brian McGoldrick; all fully certified in the Professional Ski Instructors Association. His program mimicked that of the PSIA and was in sync with cutting edge changes. In 1981, daycare was added to Buck Hill for children aged 2-5 from 9-5pm each day. The daycare was well received.

Almost everyone is having fun at ski school!

In 1982, a development team was created for young ski racers. It was founded by Frank Condon and later run by Marci Brower and Craig Opel. The program eventually included over two hundred skiers. Fast pacesetters were given handicaps whose times were chased by all-comers, just like the national NASTAR program. Participants competed for gold, silver, and bronze medals. Bloomquist and his staff offered private lessons for these aspiring racers.

Buck Hill's commitment to the development of women skiers was exemplified by a clinic held in 1984, by renowned *Ski Magazine* contributor,

Ralph Thornton interviewing Jeanne Thoren at Buck Hill.

Jeannie Thoren[*]. Jeannie was asked by a local businessman, Jim McWethey who owned the Ski Hut in Wayzata, MN, to come to Minnesota (from Sun Valley) to host a women's clinic. She was then known for her theory, she called the "Thoren Theory," in which she believed that because women were not small men, they needed specialized equipment and instruction. Jeannie fell in love with the area, and ended up hosting many clinics at Buck Hill.

By 1984, the *Minneapolis Star and Tribune* newspaper had selected Buck Hill as the best place to learn to ski in Minnesota. The school's excellence was now officially established.

1986-1993

In 1986, the next person to take over the direction of the ski school was Bobbi Sipe. Her husband Tom was already an instructor. Bobbi was business like, direct, and professional. Individual instructors were acknowledged with weekly and annual awards.

During her tenure, a major change took place in the form of snowboarding. The PSIA became the newly titled PSIA-AASI (American Association of Snowboard Instruction), and additional instructors were hired to teach the new sport. The countrywide Gradual Length Method, initiated by Cliff Taylor was also new to instruction. This concept was for beginners to first learn to slip on snow with short skis. As they became more proficient, longer skis were issued, then followed by regular length boards.

Bobbi Sipe at Buck Hill in the 1990's

The nationally franchised SKIwee program was made available for the very young learners. Buck Hill bought into it with the purchase of SKIwee banners, bibs, brochures, and report cards. Bobbi followed the annual tradition of a year end intra-ski school race with a party following, for all. Bobbi continued as the director until 1992.

1993-1994

The 1993 season welcomed Jeff Kennedy as Buck Hill's new ski school director. Jeff was a PSIA-ASSI level three examiner besides being chosen by *Ski Magazine* as one of the best one hundred ski instructors in the United States. Jeff had a good eye for a learner's successive skills and he taught his employees through graphic organization. He was always interested in learning and he adhered to the structure of the PSIA-ASSI, just like his predecessor. He gave progress cards to students as well as parents. He also had full-time instructors helping him including Phil Marick, Julie Welsh, Richard Balsley, Mark Johnson, and Barry Weinstein.

Mile Gilgan, Ted Colvin, Julie Welsh, and Craig Dow, about 1989

Sunday Development Team, 2005.

Saturday Development Team 2005 - too numerous to name.

1994 -2015

In 1994, Tom Schulz became the next ski school director. He had been a Buck Hill employee for eight years, and Tom provided a steady, consistent hand.

He had rare people skills and he led quietly, yet forcefully. Over the two-plus decades, giant changes took place. *Ski Magazine's* children's program Skiwee came to an end. Tom established the FASST Kids program to replace it. FASST, short for Fun Alpine Ski and Snowboard Teaching for Kids, housed three separate programs: Little Bucks for skiers age 4-6, Buck Hill Cruisers for skiers age 7-12, and Buck Boarders for snowboarders age 7-12. The area developed its own brand for young beginners to learn. In addition, the ever evolving and changing shapes of skis and snowboards necessitated a new learning curriculum. Tom taught his staff how to accommodate the new shapes and how to change their techniques to fit the new shapes.

Madeline and Max Wiltgen introducing the 97-98 season.

National PSIA-ASSI representatives were invited to Buck Hill to demonstrate new techniques to key instructors. The process of certification throughout its levels met on Tuesday nights with a group of examiners: Paul Aasen, Grant Nakamura, Jeff Kennedy, Larry and Vickie Berg, Justine Soine, and Tom Schulz.

Tom Schulz family - Tylee, Julie, Hannah, and Tom.

Area manager, Don McClure, lured snowboarders to the area with the installation of a large and a mini half-pipe created by a master machine that hollowed a channel in the snow. The machine was aptly named the Pipe Dragon. Buck Hill spared no expense to welcome its high flying customers. The slope once called Meadows, became a staple for boarders and its popularity snowballed. The ski school evolved as well. Young boarders and skiers could now enroll in the newly created X-Team which complemented the existing skiers' D-Team.

Jenny Stone, an accomplished snowboard instructor.

Tom realized that anything new could increase ticket sales, nothing ever stayed the same. Not only did instructors have to be trained to the established ways of skiing, they also needed to expand their skills for new innovations in both skiing and snowboarding. New instructors were required to go through the Instructor Training Program. Tom's perspective was very much like Chuck's own perspective had been - to make the guest experience as good as it could possibly be. Learning never slowed down. On Thursday nights general clinics were held. The curriculum was race course setting, gate blocking, station training for school groups, rotor pool, edging, and split level groups. The list went on and on. The instructors came away with a "bag of tricks" to bolster their lessons. Thursday night clinicians were Nate Springer, Craig Opel, Marci Brower, Grant Nakamura, Brooks Lillehei, Jon Wittman, and Tom Hayden to list a few. Over the years, many filled the role of full time staff including Mark Johnson, Harry Nielson, Dale Pierson, Jeff Johnson, Chad Schauer, Robin Davis, and Diana Drake.

Marci Brower

Under Schulz' charge, the ski school grew to over 200 instructors, and an assistant director, Diana Drake, was needed and added. She was efficient, receptive, multi-talented, and flexible. When needed, she could drop her desk duties and deliver a lesson to either skiers or snowboarders. Weekday school groups had expanded and in some cases, to three busloads of students. After passing proficiency tests, they would flood the ski runs both mornings and afternoons. Drake had played a valuable role in orchestrating this program. To prepare for this program's success, she would travel to various middle schools to explain the process to chaperones, teachers, and students.

Fun for all at Padraig's Place.

Padraig's Place began in 2008 by Brian and Eileen Foley. Having grown up skiing at Buck Hill, Eileen wanted to share the joy of skiing with her son, Padraig. Getting Padraig on the snow posed a challenge, however, as there were not many lesson options for children with special needs. This inspired Brian and Eileen to begin their own adaptive ski program, giving special families a place to enjoy winter sports in a supportive and welcoming environment. With much support from Buck Hill, Padraig's Place has continued to serve the special needs community for more than a decade. The program serves children with both cognitive and physical disabilities, providing lessons that suit the individual needs of each participant.

Padraig Foley and his dad Brian.

Two former ski school enrollees, Gaylord Gladwin and Dave Hinz, were selected to establish an adult race program to support the growing interest in adult racing leagues and NASTAR at Buck Hill. Its name is an acronym for NAtional STAndard Race, the world's largest ski race competition. It employs a handicap system based on international champions. Since its inception in 1968, millions of athletes have raced against the stopwatch at over 100 resorts that sponsor the plan. Every participant can earn a handicap which is awarded Platinum, Gold, Silver, or Bronze designations in modified giant slalom courses. Buck Hill was among the first to adopt the concept. An enclosed ramp with NASTAR emblazoned on its sides was erected on the top of Milk Run. The area created a Boot Camp to help racers hone their skills. Gaylord took the leading role in race coaching. He was passionate about the sport and, with his natural abilities and infectious personality, Boot Camp exploded. He was famous for reforming lazy, non-listeners into attentive learners. Sadly, he passed away in 2013, yet the program continued with Dave Hinz. His personality was much like Gaylord's and racers were drawn to Buck Hill. Pierce Skate and Ski Shop was one of the sponsors of the clinic.

Gaylord Gladwin, a very dedicated coach!

As time passed to the year 2000, the ski school business continued to grow and expand. The need for quality, hard-working staff in the ski school office grew as well. In 2002, the ski school was lucky to hire Barb Bakken to work as an administrator. Barb provided guests with outstanding customer service and was a joy to work with. Her diligence, professionalism, and eye for detail helped the ski school keep up with the growing demands.

Beverly Kossack, making ski school even more fun!

The Buck Hill Ski and Snowboard School has been fortunate to have such a committed staff, many of whom put in years of faithful service. The following is a list of staff members currently working that have dedicated ten or more seasons to the Buck Hill Ski and Snowboard School.

Stained glass windows in the Buckstone Lodge.

Here they are and you might say they are the backbone of our ski school. Many thanks to you all (and that includes all you instructors that came a little later) for your invaluable contribution to the success of Buck Hill.

Marci Brower	1971	Penny Antonson	1995
Brian McGoldrick	1971	Dan McHugh	1999
Tom Hayden	1973	Paul Nakanishi	1999
Dave Hinz	1975	Barb Bakken	2000
Craig Opel	1975	Beth Gray	2000
Bruce Abbe	1978	Bob Boldus	2001
Paul Aasen	1984	Dave Carlson	2001
Lee Heggen	1984	Gene Carlson	2001
Jill Meskan	1985	Kaitlin Helfenstein	2001
Grant Nakamura	1985	Peter Cers	2003
Tim Larson	1986	Kate Drusch	2003
Matthew Schafer	1986	Janice Hatlestad	2003
Dan Strehlow	1986	Andrew Scrivener	2003
Roger Hoel*	1987	Jamie Watczak	2003
Tom Schulz	1987	Jason Whelpley	2003
Marty Peterson	1988	Emma Ryan	2004
Jeffrey Serba	1988	Carl Zeilon	2004
Michael Gilgan	1991	Scott Ferry	2005
Mike Bayers	1993	Kelsey Klein	2005
Diana Drake	1994		

The Buck Hill Ski Racing Team

1965 - 2015

Early Buck Hill coaches, L to R: Walt Heustis, Jim Turnwall, Marty Hustad, and Erich Sailer.

In the fall of 1954, one of the first things Chuck Stone did after he signed the lease with Grace Whittier was to organize a Twin City high school ski training program. This was in cooperation with the Minneapolis High School Athletic Department. Chuck, Glen Stanley, and two of the city's Olympic veterans John Burton and Norm Oakvik coached students on Saturday mornings at no cost to the young skiers. The whole idea was to promote competitive ski racing in the Twin Cities. A ski racing team was a high priority for Chuck and Nancy from the very beginning. However, the Buck Hill Ski team was not organized until 1965, when the first official season of the Buck Hill Ski Racing Team began. Walter Huestis was the first head coach assisted by Buzz Bainbridge and Marty Hustad. There were twelve racers on

Nancy & Chuck Stone in their early racing days.

the team including Bill Baumgartner, Dave* and Frank* Freeman, Newt Fuller, Bill Hoffmeister, Karl Huber, Tom Jaeger, Tom Nelson, Todd Regent, Jim Shultz, and Dave Tengdin. For the 1966-1967 season the team grew in size to about 25.

In the summer of 1969, Cindy Stone and a few other Buck Hill racers attended the Red Lodge Summer Ski Racing Camp in Montana, which was owned and operated by legendary racers and coaches Erich Sailer, Pepi Gramshammer, and Anderl Molterer. Cindy knew that Buck Hill was looking for a top notch racing coach and learned Erich was currently coaching during the winter at Mt. Telemark in Cable, Wisconsin, not too far from the Twin Cities. Cindy told her father Chuck who then contacted Erich and persuaded him to come and investigate Buck Hill. Erich took one look at the hill and knew the pitch would be excellent for training young ski racers. He joined the Buck Hill Ski Team as head coach that same year in 1969. Other notable coaches during the sixties included Pepi Pittl,

Red Lodge Summer Racing Camp, June 1975. Tim Osgood, Mike Lloyd, Polly Stone, Corry Carlson, and Cindy Stone.

Coaches at Red Lodge: Ander Molterer, Pepi Gramshammer, and Erich Sailer

Billy Baumgartner, and George Neubauer.

Over the past half century, few coaches in America have had such an impact on alpine ski racing as Erich. As of 2015, he had been a junior coach for fifty-one years and coached thousands of young ski racers. These have included U.S. Ski Team members, World Cup racers, and Olympians.

1975 Ad for Red Lodge summer racing camp

During his coaching career, Erich founded four popular and effective racing programs at four different locations. These include Buck Hill, as well as ski camps at Mt. Hood, Oregon, Red Lodge, Montana, and Hintertux, Austria. Born in Telfs in Tyrol, Austria, Erich began his skiing career at an early age. As a member of the Austrian National Team from 1948 through 1952, he placed many times in International races like the Hahnenkamm and Kandahar races. He then became a ski instructor with the famous St. Anton ski school. In 1954, he came to North America as a Head Coach at the University of British Columbia in Vancouver, Canada. In 1956, he became the Assistant Ski School Director and the P.N.S.I.A. (Pacific Northwest Ski Instructors Association) examiner at Timberline Lodge, Mt. Hood, Oregon. It was at Timberline where in 1956 he co-founded his first summer race camp. Previously, summer ski racing camps had been private affairs for a select few, but the new Mt. Hood ski racing camp was made available to many more young ski racers and this served to widen the appeal of summer ski racing training.

Alan Kildow at Red Lodge Summer Racing Camp.

Enjoying a beautiful day at Red Lodge Summer Racing Camp. Lori Greely, Susan Holes, Monica McDonald, and Jessica Stone

In 1967, Erich founded his second summer ski racing camp atop Beartooth Pass outside Red Lodge, Montana. He partnered with Austrian national team members, Pepi Gramshammer from Innsbruck and Anderl Molterer from Kitzbuhel, who won two medals at the 1956 Cortina d'Ampezzo Olympics. The camp was very successful for many years, and was easily reachable from the midwest. Red Lodge offered four ten day sessions allowing 700 athletes to train during the summer months, and was the largest ski camp in the country. In 1977, due to

1950's picture at Timberline, Mt. Hood, Oregon. L to R: Franz Gabl, Olympic silver medalist from St. Anton, Austria; Martin Strolz, World Champion and Olympian from Lech, Austria; Pepi Gabl, Franz Gabl's brother and Erich's boss at Timberline in 1956-1959; and Erich Sailer

lack of snow in Montana, Erich opened up a ski racing camp in Hintertux, Austria. He built the camp on permanent glaciers and named it the "Erich Sailer Ski Racing Camps." His racers trained adjacent to the courses of several European national teams. The cutting-edge World Cup racers were live examples for his students. The camp at Hintertux lasted fifteen seasons until 1994. In 1993, Erich moved his main summer camp back to Timberline Lodge at Mt. Hood, Oregon where he is still director today. Erich is a U.S. Ski Association (USSA) International Master Coach and over the years has had several special assignments with the U.S. Ski Team to prepare the athletes for international competition.

His excellent coaching has earned him numerous awards. In 1998, USSA named him both "U.S. Domestic Coach of the Year" and "U.S. Development Coach of the Year." That same year, the U.S. Olympic committee awarded him "USOC Development Ski Coach of the Year." In May 2004, USSA gave Erich the Tom Reynolds lifetime Achievement Award, a lifetime award for coaches. In 2005, he was inducted into the U.S. National Ski Hall of Fame, and the Austrian consulate awarded him a medal of honor for his contributions to ski racing. His tireless devotion to training ski racers has earned him numerous fans including the Seibert's who were

Erich Sailer, expert racing style.

Erich by the plaque that bears his name at the US Ski Teams' Center of Excellence.

originally from Burnsville, MN and had two racers on the Buck Hill Ski Racing Team. Erich made such an impression on them that they made a substantial donation to the new US Ski Team Center of Excellence in Erich's honor. The state of the art training facilities cardio center now bears Erich's name. At the Salt Lake City Olympics in 2002, the entire U.S. women's quota in the slalom competition were Erich's proteges.

Although Erich's life today centers around the U.S, he still maintains close ties to Austria and he returns each year to an apartment he owns in Telfs. "The older one becomes, the more one thinks about where one's roots are," he says upon reflection. For Erich, his life work was about sharing the Austrian enthusiasm for skiing. "I am a Tyrolean", he explains, and coming from a country where skiing has a long time tradition "we have held the Austrian flag high in ski racing." Over the years, Austrians have had a tremendous influence on ski racing and it remains a highly popular sport with very enthusiastic ski racing fans. Erich is very proud of his accomplishments not only in ski racing world, but the many young ski racers going through his program who have become successful doctors, lawyers, business owners, and proud parents. As of 2015, four of his former students, Lindsey Kildow-Vonn, Julia Mancuso, Paula Moltzan, and Resi Stiegler were competing at the World Cup level.

The seventies were some very exciting times for the Buck Hill Ski Racing Team. Even though the team was just beginning, Buck Hill started sending many racers to the Junior Nationals which gave the team national recognition. The 1970-1971 season was Erich Sailer's second year as head coach. There were around 70 racers on the team, and Erich started the season by introducing the team to dryland training. Erich's wife Ursula, a gymnast who had majored in physical education in her native country of Germany, was in charge of dryland training. Dryland training became an integral part of the ski team and the racers

Chuck encouraging young ski racers at Powder Ridge in 1966

Walk-a-thon fundraiser held at Buck Hill Dryland training. L to R: Erich Sailer, Nancy Stone, Jo Sparrman, Polly Stone, Ann Anderson, Jan Lloyd, & Jessica Stone.

trained twice a week inside a gymnasium and at Buck Hill on Saturday mornings. "It takes endurance to win ski races, as well as fast reactions, sprinting, balance, timing, strong legs and stomach muscles" said Erich. These can all be achieved through dryland training. The cost to join the Buck Hill Ski Team in 1970 was $195 for 8-12 year olds and $220.00 for 13-18 year olds, and included a season pass.

Over the years the Buck Hill Ski Racing Team has produced many successful racers. In the 1970-1971 season, four Buck Hill Racers were members of the Junior National Team which headed to Mammoth Mountain in March of 1971. These included Dave Freeman, Mike Meleski, Todd Reget, and Cindy Stone. Their results were not what they hoped for, but they were the first of many to travel to the Junior Nationals for hundreds of Buck Hill racers.

The early 70's was also when Cindy Nelson, from Lutsen, Minnesota, started making a name for herself in the ski racing community. Cindy was not a Buck Hill racer but she was one of the first female ski racers from Minnesota to make the

Star Tribune photo of Erich and Cindy Stone in 1971.

1971 First Buck Hill Junior National Team. Back row: Coach George Neubauer, Mike Meleski, Coach Erich Sailer, and Dave Freeman. Front row: Todd Reget and Cindy Stone

U.S. Ski team and compete on the world stage. At age sixteen she was a member of the U.S. Ski Team and competed in her first World Cup Season. She raced in the downhill, giant slalom, and slalom events. Cindy was the first American to win a World Cup downhill. She won the race on Sunday, January 13th, 1974 in Grindelwald, Switzerland beating the current world champion Annemarie

Proell-Moser. Cindy won a bronze medal in the downhill at the 1976 Winter Olympics in Austria and was a silver medalist in the downhill at the 1982 World Championships.

Jessica Stone, 12 years old at the Central Division Championships Indianhead, March 1973.

Throughout the 70's, many of the Buck Hill Racers continued their success racing in the Midwest as well as competing in races throughout the United States. In 1972, Cindy Stone won the slalom at the Western States Championships in Aspen, Colorado by over two seconds. Mike Meleski, whom Erich at the time called "The most talented racer I have ever coached," won silver at the 1973 North American Alpine slalom Championships in Crystal Mountain, Washington. The winner of the race was Phil Mahre who later in his career, was a three time Olympian, winning two Olympic (gold and silver) medals in slalom.

During the mid 70's, many more Buck Hill racers dominated the races throughout the Midwest. Kevin Arms, Cory Carlson, Jim Holst, Barry Jaeger, Stephanie LeMay, Mike, Judy and Sue Lloyd, Jessica Stone, and Dave Tengdin were all placing in the top 10. Jessica won the slalom and giant slalom at the

1972 Junior National Team. Back row, L to R: Coach Erich Sailer, Cory Carlson, Dave Tengdin, Kevin Arms, Mike Lloyd, and Coach Pepi Pittl. Bottom row: Cindy Stone, Jim Holst, Tom Lowe, and Wade Arms.

twelve and under divisional championships at Schuss Mountain, Michigan in 1973. Cindy Stone continued with her success and won the Minnesota Coca Cola Cup in 1974 and Kevin Arms won the Cup in the Men's division. The Minnesota Coca Cola cup is presented to the outstanding male and female alpine ski racer in the state of Minnesota based upon season long performance in Elite and Senior Alpine sanctioned races held in Region I, C.U.S.S.A. (Central United States Skiing

1983 Buck Hill Invitational

Susan Holes, Kristy Gartner, Lori Greely, and Coach Alan Kildow at a race in Winter Park, CO.

Association). Throughout the 1970's, the popularity of ski racing in the midwest continued to grow and Buck Hill was one of the reasons for this growth. Chuck Stone was always an enthusiastic supporter of ski racing. In 1973, Chuck felt that it would be nice to host a "homecoming" race for Region One alumni who were away at college but would be home for the holidays. It would also allow the local regional competitors to have a "scored" race before the national points list update on January 1st. He spoke with USSA officials and got the race on the calendar and named it the Buck Hill Christmas Race. Held annually on December 23rd, the race has had great success and it continues to this day. The top seed traditionally included U.S. Ski Team members, elite college team members, as well as top local and foreign competitors. In 1981, local elite competitor Ara Burrell was tragically killed in an airplane accident and the Buck Hill Christmas Race was re-named the "Ara Burwell Memorial." After Chuck Stone's death in 1994, the race was again re-named as the "Chuck Stone Memorial Race." The race continues today as the marquis national point race in the region and the entire Central Division.

In 1975, Buck Hill sent seven racers to the USSA North American Junior Alpine

Buck Hill Ski Team, 1972.

Championships at Big Mountain in Whitefish, Montana. Kevin Arms, Cory Carlson, Jim Holst, Mike Lloyd, Cindy Stone, and Dave Tengdin all competed.

In 1976, Erich hired two new coaches, Alan Kildow, former junior national champion, and Jim Holst, a former Buck Hill Ski Racer. That same year, Cindy Stone and Mike Meleski continued their ski racing careers in college, both receiving full athletic scholarships at Division 1 ski racing schools. Mike went off to the University

Joining the team in 1975, Andrzej Derezinski became an invaluable addition to the coaching staff.

of Wyoming where he won the NCAA Slalom Championship. Cindy headed to the University of New Mexico where she placed second in the NCAA Campionships in Red River, NM. Buck Hill racers would go on to win four NCAA Slalom Championships: Mike Meleski in 1976, Biere Marceau in 1984, Sterling Grant in 2011, and Paula Moltzan in 2017.

Lori Greely, another Buck Hill ski racer, was named to the U.S. Ski Team's developmental squad in 1978 when she was only 14. Erich always considered her his first of many athletes to make the U.S. Ski Team. Lori lived in Kimball, MN which is about 100 miles from Buck Hill. Her father Ron Greely was general manager of Powder Ridge Ski Area at that time. Lori would travel to Buck Hill from St. Cloud to train with Erich along with Susan and Shawn Holes, who were also on the Buck Hill team. The following year in 1979, both Lori and Susan were named to the U.S. Ski Team.

Accomplished Buck Hill Racers, from L to R: Barry Jaeger, Cory Carlson, Colby Lund, Tom Nelson, Ann Freeman.

At the 1978 Minnesota State High School Championship, Buck Hill Ski racers took the top three spots in both the men's and women's races. Doug Tengdin was first, Bruce Yonehiro was second, and Peter Kness was third. Mary Boss was first for the women, Monica McDonald was second, and Marcia Lyman was third. Over the years, Buck Hill racers have won many state championships including Andrea Saterbak, Claire Abbe, Joe Sipe, and Dillion Thomas, all of whom won 2 state titles. Only three ski racers have ever won the Minnesota State High School Championships three times and two of them were Buck Hill racers: Nelson Carlson and Nicole Larson, the only female racer ever to win three times.

The 1980's were very successful years for Buck Hill racers. Jeff Kastner competed in the 1981 Junior Olympics I in Squaw Valley along with Biere Marceau and Andrea Saterbak. Brad Kastner, Jeff's younger brother, competed in the Junior Olympics III at Pico Peak, VT. Brad was ranked first in his age group nationally for slalom. David Gartner, Jeff Dekko, and Kaari Simonson also competed at the Junior Olympics II in Incline Village, Nevada. Brooks Chandler, Heidi Hensel, Tori Lowe (from the Ski Hut Team), and Jessica Stone were all members of a winning University of Minnesota's alpine team. Also in 1981, Cory Carlson, Lori Greely, and Tony Olin competed on the Europa Cup Tour which is the World Cup satellite tour.

Cory Carlson

In 1982, Cory Carlson was selected to be on the United States Alpine Ski Team. Cory started racing at Buck Hill when he was nine, and became one of Erich's first proteges. Cory won the 1976 Minnesota State Championship when he was in 9th grade, one of the youngest state champions in Minnesota history. Cory also won many regional races in the Midwest which caught the eye of the U.S. Ski team coaches. Cory was invited to train in Austria and Switzerland for four weeks with the US Ski Team and, after twelve time trials, was selected for the team. Cory spent ten years on the US Ski team, and had a few World Cup starts. Some of Cory's U.S. Ski Team friends came to Buck Hill for the Chuck Stone Memorial Race in 1982. Tiger Shaw (Now CEO of the US Ski Team) from Manchester, NH and Felix McGrath from Stowe,

L to R: Tiger Shaw, Cory Carlson, and Felix McGrath at the Buck Hill Invitational

VT thought racing at Buck Hill would be a breeze because of the small size but they were defeated by Cory on his home hill. "Everyone on the team knows about Buck Hill," Carlson said. "It's a big joke but all of the guys on the National Team respect me for coming from a small ski area like this." In 1983, Cory won a Europa Cup Slalom in Italy and was 8th in a World Cup Slalom in Sweden. Cory continued his racing into his late 20's and raced on the U.S. Pro Ski Tour. Cory had many corporate sponsors including American Airlines, Seagrams, and Century Travel.

Cory also had a contract with ESPN to do all of the Super Series events as well as help out with their other broadcasts. Cory continued his passion for skiing into his career which has centered around skiing, color commentary for the World Cup and hospitality. He is Director of Sales and Marketing at the Four Season Hotel and Resorts in Jackson Hole, Wyoming.

All great racers, The Tengdin Boys: DJ, Doug, and Dave.

In 1984, Buck Hill Ski Team member Biere Marceau won the gold medal in slalom at the NCAA championships at Attitash in New Hampshire. This was quite an accomplishment for a skier from the midwest. Biere beat two Norwegian racers who were fresh off the World Cup. Eight of the top 10 finishers were Europeans. In 1984, Buck Hill also sent many racers to the Subaru Cup, a Nor-Am at Snow King Resort in Jackson Hole, WY. The racers were Anne Buckley, Monica McDonald, Kaari Simonson, and Polly Stone. Also in 1984, Polly won the Caruther's Cup, which is based on points accumulated in races over the course of the season, and was selected to compete in the Junior Olympics for ages 16-18 at Crystal Mountain, Washington. Other Buck Hill team members competing were Greg Bradbury, Anne Buckley, and David Gartner. Greg Bradbury was ranked fourth in the country in his age group for slalom and David Gartner was ranked fifth. Buck

Polly Stone racing at the Jr. Olympics at Big Mountain, MT.

Polly Stone holding the Carruther's Cup.

Hill racers Kiki Bailey and Polly Stone were also selected to compete in the 1985 Junior Olympics at Mount Snow, Vermont.

Joe Levins and Tim Hanson, both Buck Hill Ski Team members, were named to the US Alpine Training Ski Team in 1988. After racing on the Buck Hill team for many years they both enrolled at Burke Mountain Academy. Erich Sailer commented on their success: "Buck Hill made them, now the East Coast claims them. It robs our Central

Joe Levins racing at Crested Buttle, CO.

Division of it's deserved recognition and of qualifying spots in the nationals... Tim Hanson is the most motivated skier I've ever coached. He never stops, and keeps on practicing." *The Denver Post* wrote an article on Joe and Tim in February of 1991 after they placed 1st and 3rd at the National Alpine Championships at Crested Butte. Joe was the first ever Men's champion from Minnesota. Joe was also named to the 1994 Olympic Team, the second Minnesotan ever to be named to a U.S. Olympic Alpine Team.

In January of 1989, Gregg Wong interviewed Erich for an article in the *St. Paul Pioneer Press* about racers leaving the Midwest to race in the mountains. Erich has always believed skiers can get all the training and coaching they need from Buck Hill. According to Erich "Skiers don't have to leave the Midwest and the Central Division to succeed. It's harder to do it from here, but it can be done. And it is much less expensive. We do everything possible to give the skiers every opportunity to succeed. If they have the talent, motivation and equipment, they can succeed from here as well as from anywhere else. My philosophy is to make excellent technical slalom skiers. Then once they make the U.S. Ski Team in slalom, they have the foundation and opportunity to learn giant slalom and

Martina Sailer racing downhill at age 10 in Aspen, CO.

L to R: Martina, Erich, and Ursula Sailer at the Chuck Stone Memorial Ski Race.

Martina Sailer

downhill."

1989 was a big year for the Buck Hill Ski Team. Erich and Ursula's daughter, Martina, was starting to make a name for herself and in 1989 won the ten and under skiing title at the USSA Central Division Championships in Pine Mountain, Michigan. That was Martina's second time winning that title and she was ranked number one in the country in her age group in slalom. Kristina Koznick and Tasha Nelson were also becoming nationally recognized with their strong results. Kristina won two F.I.S downhills at Keystone and Tasha was third in two slaloms at Steamboat. Both girls were ranked number one in their age groups in slalom and Kristina was also ranked number one in giant slalom. Also in 1989, Tony Olin placed third at two F.I.S. slaloms and Jamie Engleking, Eric Lempke, and Ellie Levins were also getting good race results. At the 1989 Buck Hill Invitational, Tim Hanson and Joe Levins both competed and Cory made an appearance as well. Joe won the men's race and Kristina Koznick won the women's race.

The success the Buck Hill Ski Team achieved in the 70's and 80's continued into the 90's. In 1990, Erich Sailer was at the helm as the head coach along with assistant coaches Greg Hall, Barry Jaeger, Brad Kastner, Mike Larkin, Colby Lund, Tony Olin, Kurt Reichert, and Mark Thatcher. Although the Buck Hill Ski Racing Team had great success in 1989, Eric was always pushing the Team to greater heights. The objectives for the 1990 season were:

Chuck Stone winners from L to R: Tony Olin, Joe Levins, and Morgan Burns

A partial view of the Buck Hill Ski Racing Team Wall of Fame.

1. Provide a structured program, so that each individual athlete can reach his or her full potential in

competitive skiing.

2. Provide the opportunity to grow physically and emotionally in the environment of their parents' homes.
3. Upgrade ski racing in our town, our hill, our division and put some of our racers on the U.S. Ski Team.
4. Provide all this without having to move away from home, the guidance of the parents, and still have a choice of schools.
5. Provide the best coaching possible, and still not discriminate against the less privileged. In fact the team is a non-profit undertaking for Buck Hill.
6. Keep their future and education in mind always. Work with universities and colleges to give some of our racers the opportunity of a ski scholarship.

Elizabeth Hoigaard, another Buck Hill racer, won the Minnesota State slalom title in February of 1990. Elizabeth also qualified to compete in the Nor Am races in New Hampshire, along with Tasha Nelson. Buck Hill racer Jamie Engleking was the winner of the boys state title.

Prior to Lindsey Kildow, the Buck Hill Ski Racing Team member who achieved the most success in the U.S. and internationally was Kristina Koznick. Kristina stayed with the Buck Hill Team throughout her entire career. Kristina starting racing on the Buck Hill Team when she was just six years old and eventually became a World Cup slalom champion and competed in three Olympics. At age six, Kristina's dad Jeff was picking her up at Buck Hill after a day of skiing and could not find her, only to locate her in the video game room. Her father immediately enrolled Kristina in our developmental ski team program...and the rest is history! She was fifteen when she represented the United States in the World Junior Championships. At the time, she was the youngest US skier to have done that. She was quoted in a *Ski Racing* article at age fifteen talking about skiing in the Midwest "Well, it is not like the East or the West where kids travel all over the place. In the Midwest, everybody knows each other, so it's really close. Mostly they are all very supportive." 1991 was when Kristina really started to be noticed. She was sixth in the U.S. Alpine Championship slalom after starting number 33. In 1992, Kristina started racing on the Europa Cup. She had a second and a ninth place finish in the slaloms.

In January of 1992,

Kristina Koznick

Kristina Koznick

Kristina was on the U.S. Ski Team's regional squad and spent the majority of her time racing in Europe. In 1993, Kristina started racing in World Cups as well as the Europa Cup. She was the number one ranked slalom skier in her age group in the country and at age seventeen was the youngest member of the U.S. Ski Team. In 1994, Kristina was injured and did not qualify for the Olympics but 1995 was a great year for Kristina. She won a Europa Cup slalom in Bergen, Germany and continued racing on the World Cup Circuit where she was the top U.S. finisher. Kristina also won the slalom at the U.S. Alpine Championships three times, in 1995, 1996 and 1997.

In March of 1996, Gregg Wong wrote an article in the *St. Paul Pioneer Press* about Kristina's call to Erich Sailer when she was having a rough season. She had a back injury and frost bitten toes and was not skiing to her potential. "It was a really discouraging year. I was going through the motions. Nothing was happening." Kristina called home and her father Jeff suggested she call Erich. Kristina said, "I told Erich this was the worst I've ever skied and asked him if there was anything he could tell me. We just talked about skiing in general, about the things I have heard from him since I was eight years old. He gave me some drills to try and told me to go free skiing the next day." A few days after speaking with Erich she finished eleventh in the slalom World Cup at Mammoth Mountain, her best World Cup finish of the winter. She finished the season by winning the U.S. Alpine slalom championships by 1.63 seconds. "To say I owe it to that phone call to Erich would be an understatement," Koznick said. "I've had four great races since then, and now I'm eager to get to another season and especially to the Olympics."

1998 was an Olympic year and Kristina started out winning the first World Cup slalom of the season in Are, Sweden. She went on to have three top World Cup finishes. There was a lot of press about Kristina because it was an Olympic year. She was featured in a *New York Times* article on January 5th about how her positive thoughts were leading to positive results. Kristina is quoted as saying "I write down what I want to accomplish for the day, but most of what I write down is just a reminder of why I am here and how much I like myself as a person. And when I leave my room to face the world, I leave in a great mood." Kristina is one of the most accomplished

50 times World Cup winner, Alberto Tomba (AKA The Italian Stallion) and Kristina Koznick take time to chat at Buck Hill during the Lexus Tomba tour, presented by Rossignol in 2000..

and decorated ski racers to come out of the Buck Hill Ski racing team. She retired in 2006 with six World Cup slalom wins, 20 World Cup podiums, and placing second twice in the overall World Cup title for slalom in 1998 and 2002. Kristina was also the top rated American slalom racer in the world for four years in a row. In 2015, Kristina Koznick was inducted into the U.S. Ski Team Hall of Fame. Most articles mentioned her humble beginnings and those were of course at Buck Hill. We were all very proud of Kristina's many accomplishments and her loyalty to the Buck Hill Ski Racing Team.

More and more articles on Buck Hill ski racing program began to appear on the national level, mainly because of the great success of many of the Buck Hill racers. In November of 1991, *Ski Magazine* featured an article titled **Happy to be Small** written by Nicholas Howe, about three small ski areas, Buck Hill being one of them. The article states that racing has always been a drawing card for Buck Hill. Jean-Claude Killy began his pro winning streak here in 1973. Joe Levins, the top slalom racer on the U.S. Ski Team got his start here and last year the program had the top three under-18 slalom racers in the country. In March of 1992, *Ski Magazine* published an article titled **Big Little Buck** by Reade Bailey. The article focused on how Erich turned Buck Hill into the legendary capital of American ski racing. In the article, Reade points out that Buck Hill has produced eight U.S. Ski Team members and nine collegiate champions and this was just the beginning. The article gives a great description of what goes on at Buck Hill on a typical training day. Chuck Stone is quoted as saying, "It's a bamboo jungle out there." Reade points out that one of the main reasons Buck Hill can produce such great slalom skiers is the amount of runs they can take on a typical training session. The old fashioned rope tow is the preferred method of transportation. In 30 seconds you can be at the top of the hill which allows you to get in 30-40 runs during practice, which is something you can't do in big mountains.

In March of 1992, Martina Sailer won the giant slalom, tied for first in the Super G, and was second in slalom to take the overall title at the Junior Olympics

Coach Tony Olin with DJ Tengdin

Coach Brad Kastner with racer Wyatt Wiltgen

III in Winter Park, Colorado. According to Erich "Winning a giant slalom was unbelievable, considering that we mostly produce slalom skiers in the Midwest. But even more impressive is that she won a Super-G."

In 1993, Tony Olin was named head coach of the Buck Hill Ski Racing Team. Erich's new title was Program Director. In 1994, Martina Sailer was ranked number one in slalom and number two in giant slalom among fifteen year olds in the United States. *The St. Paul Pioneer* press featured an article written by Greg Wong about Martina and Erich. Erich is quoted as saying, "I've not coached anybody like her. That's not only because she is my daughter but also because she has intelligence, she works hard, and she has the talent. I could see it when she was nine years old. I could see that she was going to be good." Martina had won every race she entered in the Midwest, including six Mid-Ams that season. She also qualified for the Canadian Nationals, the Nor-Ams and the Junior Olympics.

Some other Buck Hill racers doing very well in 1994 were Daniel Dalseth, Ellie Levins, and Jeff Trastek. Ellie was second in the J1 women's slalom at Attitash, New Hampshire and Daniel won the men's slalom. Jeff won the men's combined title at the Rolex Rocky Mountain Central JIII Olympics at Winter Park, CO.

1995-96 was another great season for the Buck Hill Ski Racing team. The coaching staff for the 1995-96 season was Erich Sailer, Pascal Dalseth, Erik Gabrielson, Greg Hall, Brad Kastner, Mike Larkin, Erik Lempke, Colby Lund, Truck Morrison, Tony Olin, and Maria Schilling. Many Buck Hill racers were competing at the national level. Kristina placed eleventh at the first World Cup slalom of the season and Martina was competing in the Nor-Ams. Other Buck Hill racers had the opportunity to compete in the Colorado Ski Games. Holly Beaulieu, Chip Davenport, John Hovde, John Simmons, and Nick Tongen all raced at several sites. Holly also won the Minnesota High School State Championships in 1996.

The 1995 Buck Hill Chuck Stone Memorial Ski Race was dominated by current and past Buck Hill Ski team members. Kristina won the race, Martina was second, followed by Maria Schilling. Jennifer Dahl, Kristen Hayden, and Kristen Kolkmann all finished in the top 15. Jamie Engleking, a former Buck Hill Racer skiing for the University of Colorado, won the men's slalom and Adam Barron was third. Daniel Dalseth, skiing for Dartmouth College, was seventh and another former Buck Hill Racer Jon Adsem was 13th.

In 1996, the cost of the Buck Hill Ski Racing Team was $1,325 including a season pass, quite an increase from 1970. The team was going strong with over 100 team members and plenty of opportunities to develop the best ski racers. There was comprehensive dry land training, a fall ski camp at Winter Park, CO as well as a Christmas camp at Buck Hill. The Buck Hill racers continued to be very successful in the 1996-1997 season. Tasha Nelson was ranked number three in the country for slalom and finished in the top ten in some important races. Joe Sipe was ranked number one in the country for slalom for 14 year olds and eleven year old Lindsey Kildow was starting to make a name for herself.

Many Buck Hill racers headed to the Junior Olympics in March of 1996. The JII boy racers were Chip Davenport, John Hovde, Jon Simmons, Nick Tongen with Chip placing second in the slalom. The girls were represented by Holly Beaulieu and Torrey Tobin. At the JIII's, representing Buck Hill were Lindsey Kildow, Mary Lasse, Joe Sipe, Kyle Vassislopoulos, and Mike Woell. Kyle was fourth in the men's slalom and Lindsey was second in the women's slalom. Nelson Carlson, Case Edgeton, and Graham Irving all went to the JIV's and took home five medals. Graham took a third in Super G, second in giant slalom, and won the All Terrain. Nelson placed third in the giant slalom and third in the slalom.

Coach Doug Nordmeyer holds drylands training at the Air Force Wing.

In January of 1997, there was an article by Pete Temple about the Buck Hill Ski Racing Team in the local Burnsville paper. The article summed up nicely all the accomplishments the team had achieved since inception, including putting ten racers on the U.S. Ski team and 22 racers receiving major college scholarships. In the past ten years, Buck Hill had claimed 33 gold medals, 25 silver, and 15 bronze at the Junior Olympics and Junior Nationals. The article also talks about the great coaching staff at Buck Hill. Erich is quoted as saying, "Ninety-five percent of my coaches have been members of the Buck HIll Ski Racing Team so they know how I like it." In the same paper, there was an article about the up and coming racers who performed well at the Chuck Stone Memorial Race in December of 1997. One of those racers was Lindsey Kildow, who finished nearly a second ahead of her closest competitor. Even back then her coaches knew she was special.

Tony Olin is quoted as saying, "She is just phenomenal. She's really the best skier we have seen at this age." Jamie Engleking, a former Buck Hill Racer who was skiing for the University of Colorado Boulder, competed in the World University Games in Muju, South Korea. There were over 1600 athletes from 49 nations competing in these games. Jamie was selected as one of the five male US alpine athletes to compete in this event. He competed in the downhill, Super G, giant slalom, and slalom.

Kaylin Richardson and Lindsey Kildow at the Chuck Stone Memorial.

The American men's alpine team was the best all around squad at the World University Games followed by Slovenia and then Italy.

Another Buck Hill Ski Racing Team member who achieved great success was Tasha Nelson. Tasha learned to ski at Powder Ridge where her parents were ski patrollers. She started racing at Buck Hill when she was eight years old and after coaching her for two years Erich knew she was special. Erich said of Tasha "She was always the first to practice and the last to leave. She worked extremely hard." In 1989 when Tasha was fifteen, she qualified for the Nor-Am series races at Attitash, New Hampshire and Stratton, Vermont. Aside from the World Cup races and the U.S. National Championships, these are the most important races held in North

L to R: Kristina Koznick, Tasha Nelson, Erich Sailer, and Martina Sailer

America. She did not have any FIS points so she had to start last. At Attitash Tasha did not make the cut but she fared better at Stratton. She was 42nd overall in the first slalom after starting 81 and 49th overall in the second slalom. Tasha also won the slalom at the Junior Olympics in March of 1989.

Tasha continued to ski well throughout the nineties but was sidelined with some knee injuries. In February of 1997, Tasha was the top ranked slalom skier in the country and had already qualified for the 1998 Olympics. She started out the season ranked 69th in the world in slalom and worked her way up to 33rd. Tasha accomplished all of this after three knee surgeries and being out of the sport for three years. She also placed 13th at the World Alpine Championships in Sestri, Italy in February of 1997.

1998 was an Olympic year and Tasha was headed to the Olympics in

Tasha Nelson, 1998 Olympics, Nagano, Japan.

Nagano, Japan with fellow Buck Hill racer Kristina Koznick. She was featured in an article by Rachel Blount in the *Minneapolis Star Tribune* in 1998. Tasha was quoted as saying about being in the Olympics "It's incredible. It took me a long time to come back from the injuries, but I did it because I hadn't reached my potential. I didn't want to be watching the Olympics this year. I wanted to be there." The *Minneapolis Star Tribune* featured Tasha and Kristina in another article by Rachel Blount in February of 1998 titled **Bucking Tradition**. The article touched on Tasha's friendship with Kristina and how they had been talking about being in the Olympics since they were young racers at Buck Hill. Unfortunately, Tasha was disqualified in her first run of the Women's Olympic slalom. Kristina was 8th after the first run and skied out in the second run.

Lindsey Kildow at the start of the 2002 Salt Lake City Winter Olympics.

In 1999, Lindsey Kildow, a Buck Hill racer until the age of 13, became the first American athlete to win the "Cadets" slalom events in Italy's Trofeo Topolino di Sci Alpino. In 1986, Lindsey's hero Picabo Street participated but did not medal in the same Topolino event. In 1995, Lindsey first met Street in person a few years later. Street said she was stunned watching 15-year-old Lindsey ski for the first time in 1999. She marveled at Vonn's knack for following the fall line. "The faster she went, the bigger the smile on her face," Street said. "You can't teach somebody to love the fall line like that little girl loved the fall line." After climbing through the ranks of the U.S. Ski Team, she made her World Cup debut at age sixteen on November 18, 2000, in Park City, Utah. The most successful American ski racer of all time, and now the most successful woman ski racer in the world. Lindsey Kildow started her racing career at Buck Hill in 1993 when she was nine years old. Polly Stone Hanson was the first female coach for the Buck Hill Ski Racing Team and was one of Lindsey's early coaches. Lindsey was part of the program until her family moved to Colorado in the late nineties.

Young Lindsey Kildow at Buck Hill.

Young Lindsey making some turns at Buck Hill, wearing her Ewe First hat.

In her Olympic debut at the 2002 Winter Olympics in Salt Lake City at age seventeen, Lindsey raced in both slalom and the combined, with her best result coming in sixth in combined. On March 4, 2003, she earned a silver medal in downhill in the Junior World Championship at Puy Saint-Vincent, France. On March 24, 2004, Lindsey was the downhill silver medalist at the U.S. Alpine Championships at Mt. Alyeska Resort in Girdwood, Alaska. Earlier that year, Vonn climbed onto the World Cup podium for the first time with a third-place finish in downhill at Cortina d'Ampezzo, Italy. Her maiden victory in that specialty came at Lake Louise, Alberta, in December 2004. She captured five more World Cup podiums over the next two months.

At her second Winter Olympics in 2006, Vonn clocked the second-best time in the first practice run yet crashed in the second training run for the downhill race on February 13, 2006, in San Sicario, Italy. She was evacuated by helicopter to Turin and was hospitalized overnight. Despite a bruised hip and strong pains, she returned to the slopes two days later to compete and finished in eighth place. The gritty performance earned her the U.S. Olympic Spirit Award, as voted by American fans, fellow Team USA athletes, former U.S. Olympians, and members of the media for best representing the Olympic Spirit.

Lindsey's third Olympics were the Vancouver Winter Olympics in 2010. Lindsey planned to compete in all five women's alpine events. On February 10, she revealed she had severely bruised her shin in training the previous week. Vonn said the pain from her injury was "excruciating" and she would have a difficult time competing at the Winter Olympics. Due to unseasonably warm weather and resultant poor snow conditions, many of the Alpine skiing events were moved back, giving Vonn additional time to heal. On February 17, in her first event, Vonn won the gold medal in the downhill at Whistler Blackcomb, beating longtime U.S. rival Julia Mancuso by 0.56 seconds and becoming the first American woman to win Olympic gold in downhill. In her second event, the super combined, Vonn finished first in the downhill portion of the race. In the slalom portion, however, she crashed when she failed to get her ski around a right-hand gate. In her third event, the super-G, Vonn finished third behind Andrea Fischbacher and Tina Maze. Afterwards, Lindsey said she didn't ski the last part of the course as aggressively as she could have and lost the race as a result. In her fourth event, the giant slalom, fog affected visibility. Vonn crashed in her first run, resulting in a broken fourth finger and Vonn's disqualification. In her fifth event, the slalom, Lindsey lost control and straddled a gate, disqualifying her from the event.

Lindsey Vonn winning the gold in Vancouver at the 2010 Winter Olympics.

Although the ski team history ends in 2015, Lindsey retired in 2018 and we want to recognize all of her accomplishments. All in all, Lindsey attended 4 Olympics, winning 3 medals, one of which was gold. She attended 7 World Championships, winning 8 medals, two were gold. Lindsey raced on the World Cup circuit for 19 years earning 82 world cup wins (43-Downhill, 28-Super-G, 4-Giant Slalom, 2-Slaloms and 5-Super Combined). 137 world cup podiums, four overall titles, and sixteen discipline overall wins (8-Downhill, 5-super-G and 3-Super combined). ABSOLUTELY AMAZING!

At the Races

Chuck Stone racers, from left, Tague Thorson, Robbie Massie and Michael Holmberg

Christmas tradition, etched in Stone
MINNESOTA'S BUCK HILL WELCOMES MIDWEST RACERS HOME FOR THE HOLIDAYS
BY HILARY LUND

A photo from an article in Ski Racing Magazine written by Buck Hill racer Hillary Lund. L to R: Tague Thorson, Robbie Massie, and Michael Holmberg.

Lindsey is definitely the most recognized ski racer in the United States and abroad. We are proud to say Lindsey's racing career started right here at Buck Hill! Lindsey has been great to the team and over the years has shown up and spoken to the team and how much it meant to her. A couple summers ago, Lindsey held one of her all girls camps at Buck Hill. And at that time, Jessica chaired a dinner event to raise funds for the Buck Hill foundation and the Lindsey Vonn foundation. Lindsey was gracious, happy, and stayed way past her scheduled time to reunite with her childhood friends and family.

Buck Hill Ski racers continued their success into the early 2000's. Eleven Buck Hill athletes competed in the J1/J2 Junior Olympics in March of 2002 at Beaver Creek. The racers were Claire Abbe, Pat Abbe, Nelson Carlson, Casey Edgeton, Michael Holmberg, Hillary Lund, Robbie Massie, Nate Nesset, Christopher Prem, Gary Rude, Peter Sims, and Derek Stahlecker. Several of the racers had some satisfying results with Claire Abbe taking sixth in the slalom and Hillary Lund finishing fifteenth. For the men, Derek Stahlecker was eighth in the slalom, Nelson Carlson was fourth, and Christopher Prem was thirteen in the giant slalom.

Claire Abbe, who grew up in Burnsville right by Buck Hill, was introduced to skiing by her father Bruce, who was a ski instructor at the Hill. Claire won five Junior Olympic medals, including the gold in slalom as a JIII, which earned her a berth on the U.S. Whistler Cup team. She won the Minnesota state high school championships twice and during Claire's FIS career she won 24 FIS races and was on the podium 46 times. Claire attended the University of Denver (DU) on a full ski racing scholarship. During her time at DU, the team won two national championships. Claire also competed in the World University Games in Italy for the U.S. Team. After graduating from DU and racing and coaching one year with the Park City Ski Team, Claire took a position with the *SkiRacing.com* online magazine. Claire is another Buck Hill racer who took her passion of ski racing to the next level, and now she is Publisher and Chief Operating Officer of *Ski Racing* magazine.

Claire Abbe on the cover of Ski Utah Magazine

In 2003, traveling to the J4 Junior Olympics in Steamboat Springs from the Buck Hill Ski Racing Team were Andrew Fischer, Tenley Fontaine, Jamie Hornes, Elise Jaeger, Alex Larkin, Joey Nelson, and Tyler Pierce. The team was quite successful with Tyler Pierce getting three top ten finishes and Andrew Fischer placing second in one of the slaloms and two top ten finishes in giant slalom. The girls were successful as well with Jamie Horness placing third and fourth in the two slaloms and Tenley Fontaine placing fourth

Participants in the 2003 Buddy Werner Series.

and third in the slaloms and two top finishes in the giant slalom. The Buck Hill Ski Racing team also sent twelve athletes to the J3 Junior Olympics in Winter Park, Colorado: Annie Aho, Blake Barnes, Elinor Bradbury, Jake Braun, Hannah Condon, Perrie Finsand, Sterling Grant, Mitch Helmark, Blaine Lukens, Connor Lund, Alexander Prem, Alexandra Wennberg, and Ben Wexler. Sterling won the slalom and was sixth in the downhill. Hannah Condon was seventh in the ladies slalom and Connor Lund finished fifth in the men's slalom.

Sterling Grant's slalom win at the J3 Junior Olympics earned her a place on the team representing the United States at the Whistler Cup in British Columbia. The Whistler Cup is an annual international ski race that brings together the best 11-14 year old ski racers in the world. Six racers from the United States are chosen to compete in the event. The Whistler Cup has a deep history of showcasing some of the world's best young talent that eventually compete at the World Cup level. Past American winners include Will Brandenburg, Julia Mancuso, Sarah Schleper, (whose dad worked at Powder Ridge) Lindsey Kildow, and Andrew Weibrecht. Sterling proved she could compete with the best, posting impressive results in all three events. She was third in the slalom, 19th in the giant slalom and 22nd in the Super G. That was just the beginning of Sterling's many accomplishments and she demonstrated great determination just to get to Buck Hill!

Sterling Grant winning the Chuck Stone Memorial race.

She grew up in the small town of Amery, Wisconsin, which was an hour and half drive from Buck Hill. She knew training with Erich Sailer and the other coaches at Buck Hill was worth the long drive. Sterling and her mom Stephanie made the trip several times a week to train with the Buck Hill Team. Sterling went on to be a member of the U.S. Ski Team from 2006-2011. She also won the 2006 and 2011 Nor-Am slalom title and raced in many World Cups. Sterling went on

Sterling Grant (second from left), supporting the younger Buck Hill racers at Mt. La Crosse. L to R: Maisie Ide, Sterling, Madeline Wiltgen, and Laura Post.

to race for the University of Denver on a full scholarship and in 2011 won the very prestigious University World slalom title in Erzurum, Turkey. She also won the NCAA slalom championship at Stowe, Vermont that year. In 2012, she was named the Colorado Sports Alpine Woman of the Year.

Buck Hill continued to get favorable press in national publications. In the February 2003 issue of *Ski Magazine,* there was a feature article on Buck Hill written by Stephanie Pearson. The byline was "This tiny Midwestern ski area proves it doesn't take thousands of skiable acres to produce Olympic champions." The article elaborated on the success of the Buck Hill Ski Racing Team as well as it's history.

2007 Chuck Stone Winners. Boys, L to R: Michael Ankeny, Jacob Lund, and Patrick Conway Girls, L to R: Perrie Finsand, Claire Abbe, and Maisie Ide.

The early 2000's brought many great Buck Hill ski racers to the limelight. One of the more notable racers was Michael Ankeny. Michael was special to the Stone's because his grandparents, Pete and Margie Ankeny, were very close friends of theirs. Chuck and Pete were classmates at Dartmouth and they spent many fun times together skiing in Aspen where the Ankeny's had a home. Michael starting ski racing at Buck Hill when he was nine years old and by age ten he won his first local race and continued his success with many top finishes in local and regional races. In 2006, Michael was old enough to race FIS and did very well topping off his inaugural season winning both the slalom and the giant slalom at the J3 Junior Olympics in Vail, CO. At age sixteen, he was second in the giant slalom and won the slalom at the 2007 National Junior Championships held at Mt. Bachelor in Oregon. Later that same year, Michael qualified for the U.S. Nationals earning a 12th place in the slalom. The following year he went on to win the slalom at the 2008 U.S. National Championships in Sugarloaf, ME. Michael had many top finishes at the Nor-Ams, including twelve podiums, and two wins. In January of 2011, he qualified for his first World Cup race in Kitzbuehel, Austria. Michael went on to Dartmouth College and continued part time academics while still skiing for the US Ski team. Michael has since retired from ski racing, but will be remembered for his on-hill leadership, great personality, and just missing the quota for the Olympics in 2014 and 2018.

In 2005, Madeline Wiltgen, Chuck and Nancy's granddaughter, qualified along with Michael Ankeny for the Whistler Cup in British Columbia. The Whistler Cup is the top international skiing event in the world for junior racers. Over the years, many Buck Hill racers have qualified for this elite competition including

Claire Abbe, Nicole Larson, Paula Moltzan, Matt Strand, Mitch Underhill, Lindsey Kildow, and Thea Zerbe. In Madeline's first Junior Olympics she took ninth in the Super G, fifth in the giant slalom, won one slalom and tied with fellow teammate Nicole Larson for the gold medal in the second slalom race. Michael Ankeny had qualified the year before and took second in the slalom and Madeline took at fourth in the 2005 slalom. With Michael's and Madeline's strong results in the March 2006 Junior Olympics both Madeline and Michael qualified for another Whistler Cup in Whistler, British Columbia. At the Junior Olympics in 2006, Madeline qualified by finishing first in Super G, slalom, and giant slalom events and won the overall title. Michael qualified by winning both the slalom and giant slalom events. Michael ended up qualifying for the Whistler Cup four years in a row and became the first male American racer to do so. In 2006, Madeline made the podium at the Whistler Cup with a bronze medal in the slalom for the USA.

Michael Ankeny and his mom, Becky.

Michael Ankeny

The 2006-2007 season was another banner year for Buck Hill ski racers, sending 25 total athletes to the J3 and J4 Junior Olympics. The J3 (13 and 14 year olds) Junior Olympics were held in Aspen, CO and included J3 girls Kiltie Finsand, Maisie Ide, Kaitee Larkin, Nicole Larson, Laura Post, and Madeline Wiltgen. J3 boys were Dane Jensen, Jordan Skillman, Matthew Strand, Dylan Thomas, and Madison Whalen. Matthew Strand had a strong showing with a sixth in slalom, and a tenth in the giant slalom. Dylan Thomas was ninth in the downhill. For the girls, Nicole Larson

L to R: Matthew Strand, Michael Ankeny, and Madeline Wiltgen at the Sierra Whistler Cup in Vancouver

took the silver in slalom and a solid seventh in downhill. Madeline Wiltgen also had a great showing after crashing in the downhill and ending up in the hospital. She recovered but missed the Super-G and came back with a bronze in slalom and fourth in the giant slalom. The J4 girls included Chloe Burke, Madison Gartner, Amanda Larson, Paula Moltzan, and Thea Zerbe. The J4 boys included Connor Croasdale, Nick Eagon, Jack McNeill, Bradford Morrison, Jack Post, Chayden Schmitz, Jack Seedorf, Rolf Tengdin, and Mitchell Underhill.

Madeline Wiltgen and Nicole Larson tying for the gold at the J4 Junior Olympics in Winter Park, CO.

2007-2008 showed great results at all levels. Starting the season, Buck Hill Racers national age rankings included Madeline Wiltgen who was first in slalom and second in giant slalom, Nicole Larsen was ranked second in slalom and eleventh in giant slalom, Maisie Ide was fifth in slalom and sixth in giant slalom, and Laura Post seventh in slalom and fourteenth in giant slalom.

Madeline Wiltgen

In 2008, Buck Hill J3 Junior Olympic qualifiers included Colleen Cass, Kiltie Finsand, Maisie Ide, Paula Moltzan, Laura Post, and Madeline Wiltgen. In the boys division, Buck Hill sent Brett Bremer, Tom Grojean, Jack McNeill, Chaden Schmitz, Rolf Tengdin, and Madison Whalen. Madison took fourth in the slalom and was tenth overall. That year at the J3 Junior Olympics, Buck Hill was represented by Brett Bremer, Colleen Cass, Kiltie Finsand, Tom Grojean, Jack McNeill, Lars Midthun, Paula Moltzan, Laura Post, Chaden Schmitz, Rolf Tengdin,

Maisie Ide

Matt Strand in 2007

Buck Hill racers at the 2010 Chuck Stone Memorial Race. L to R: Laura Post, Chloe Burke, Kiltie Finsand, Maisie Ide, and Madeline Wiltgen

Madison Whalen, and Madeline Wiltgen. In the slalom, Paula won, Madeline was third, and Laura Post was seventh. In giant slalom, Paula won, Madeline was fourth, Kiltie fifth, and Laura eighth. Madeline also scored a silver medal in the Super-G. For the men, Madison was fourth in slalom, ninth in giant slalom and seventh in Super-G. At the J4 Junior Olympics in Winter Park, Buck Hill had a strong showing. Thea Zerbe won two slaloms and a fourth in giant slalom. Chloe Burke scored a fourth and a ninth in the slaloms, and Keller Hickok took ninth in the slalom. Paula won the overall title that year and Madeline was third overall.

In April of 2008, the Buck Hill Ski Racing Club was selected to receive two USSA organizational awards. The 2008 Club of the Year Award and the 2008 Alpine Club of the Year Award. These awards represent the single highest honors in the organization. The nomination information included high praise for the program and this is what was written about the Club and Erich. "The success of the Buck Hill Ski Racing Club junior athletes over the years has been consistent with very few valleys in their performance levels. Buck Hill is on a roll this 2007-2008 season and appears to be stronger than ever. Buck Hill's success is due in large part to the efforts of the Program Director, Erich Sailer. The system that Erich has installed over the years is very important. Erich usually hires alumni of the team or former World Cup athletes, bringing that important perspective to the junior realm. Thus, most staff have participated and benefited from the system as junior racers, know the system, believe in the system, and are dedicated to giving something back to the sport of ski racing and the current members of the club."

In the 2009-2010 season, nineteen racers from the Buck Hill Ski

Buck Hill Team Photo

2008 Buck Hill J4 Junior Olympic Team.

Racing Club qualified for the J3 Junior Olympics in Vail, Co. On the girls side, Buck Hill sent Mary Arndt, Chloe Burke, Marlee Gartner, Megan Greiner, Tessa Ide, Amanda Larson, Montana Mazario, Christina Nelson, Erin Olejnik, Jessica Reinhart, and Hailee Warnke. Montana won the slalom, took seventh in the giant slalom, and third in the downhill. Jessica scored a fifth in the Super-G, Chloe took eighth in the giant slalom, Marlee was seventh in the slalom, while Erin was tenth in the slalom. On the boys side, Buck Hill sent Connor Croasdale, Keller Hickok, Bradford Morrison, Vy Nguyen, Jack Post, and Griffin Struyk. Connor had a great week taking second in the downhill, fourth in slalom and fifth in the Super-G. Jack was third in the slalom, Kyle was fifth, and Bradford took tenth.

2010 Chuck Stone Winners, L to R: Michael Ankeny, Matt Strand, Jacob Lund, Jessica Reinhart, Maisie Ide, and Laura Post

Mid Am Series winners. L to R: Paula Moltzan, Maisie Ide, and Madeline Wiltgen.

2011 and 2012 brought some great results across the board. At the J3 Junior Olympics, Tommy Anderson won the slalom and Peter Kiesel placed third and Rosie Hust was fifth in the women's slalom. At the J4 Junior Olympics in Steamboat, Nellie Ide placed third in slalom and fourth in the giant slalom. Kaitlyn Vesterstein scored a fourth and fifth in the giant slaloms and placed second in the super-G. Chloe Townsend scored a pair of sixth place finishes in each of the slaloms. The boys faired well too with Andrew Shindeman placing third in the giant slalom and fifth

Paula Moltzan racing at the Junior Worlds in Jasna, Slovakia.

in the slalom. Jackson Zilverberg was sixth in the slalom and Zack Dekko was eighth in the slalom.

The first annual D.J. Tengdin Memorial Race was held March 3-4, 2012 after he died tragically the previous year. D.J. (David John) joined the Buck Hill Ski Racing Team as a seven year old and went on to be an accomplished ski racer. D.J. was a four year member of the Central A Team, a 2-time All-American, and he led the St. Olaf team to their first ever National Championship in 1988. D.J. also was the slalom champion at the 1987 Argentine National Championships. Ski racing remained close to his heart; wherever he lived he continued to race in the Masters events through North America and Europe. Within Masters, he was named to the USSA Masters National Team three times, and was the National Champion in all events a total of six times. D.J. was an inspiring racer who will be missed by all.

D.J. Tengdin, always happy to be on the slopes.

It was during this time, Paula Moltzan, who's mom and dad were Buck Hill ski instructors, started her rise to ski racing fame. Paula, who won many local and Junior Championships, started racing on the Nor-Am circuit with great results and the US Ski Team took notice. In 2013, she got her first World Cup start in Aspen, CO. As we are finishing up this book Paula's future looks bright. In February of 2015 at the FIS Alpine World Ski championships in Beaver Creek, Paula placed twentieth in the slalom. Then in March, a month later, she won gold in the slalom at the Junior World Championships at Hafjell, Norway. She was the first American woman ever to do so.

The 2013-2014 season Buck Hill sent the following to the U14 championships (formally known as the Junior Olympics) Becca Devine, Bailey Donovan, Joshua Doolittle, Jack Folkman, Izak Holfstad, Amiina Ingah, Kathryn Kossack, Aaron Kuznik, Gabriel Lessard, Lauren Nida, Isaiah Nelson (Buck Hill Olympian Tasha Nelson's nephew), Katherine Nelson, Deirdre O'Neil, John Tyler

Minnetonka's state bound boys in 2012. L to R: Matt Sinderson, Grant Bremer, Brett Bremer, Sam Bumstad, Steve Weichmann, and Nick Eagon in front.

Buck Hill parents at the state meet. L to R: Truck Morrison, Heidi* and Dave Hust.

Paula Moltzan

Louis Nguyen wins the race.

Olson, Hanna Rost, Sam Shideman, Romeo Sweeney, Mason Thorpe, Andrew Weigel, and Molly Zeller. Bailey took fifth in slalom one, ninth in slalom two, and seventh in the kombi. The boys faired a bit better with Sam placing seventh and tenth in slalom, Andrew placing sixth in slalom, and Mason scoring a ninth in the kombi. Isaiah had a great week with a second and third in the slaloms, and a first and second in the giant slalom and a second in the Super-G.

At the 2014 U-16 Championships at Howelsen Hill in Steamboat, Buck Hill racers took all three top spots, as shown in the photo from the *Steamboat Today* newspaper. Louis Nguyen won the race followed by Jack Lindsay and Tommy Anderson.

David Chodounsky is another very successful Buck Hill racer who was on the team in the early 90's then moved to Crested Butte, Colorado. David was co-captain of the Dartmouth Ski Team that won the NCAA Championships in 2007. He was also National Slalom Champion in 2005 and 2009. In 2014, David was a member of the U.S. Olympic Team that competed in Sochi, Russia. Its certainly possible that David's early training on the Buck Hill team contributed to his success as a great ski racer.

In early February of 2015, the Buck Hill Team once again made a very impressive showing at the Minnesota State High School Meet at Giants Ridge. In the boys race, Elliott Bowman was first and Peter Kiesel was second. Rosie Hust was second and Nellie Ide was third in the girls race. Mid-February of 2015, Paula Moltzan was second in both slalom and the giant slalom at the U.S. Nationals. Paula was 20th in the slalom at the World Championships at Beaver Creek also held in February. Maisie Ide, racing for Dartmouth College at the Dartmouth Skiway, won the Winter Carnival Slalom in February of 2015. Maisie won many other college races in those days and that was not an easy task. The competition at the college races was fierce. She may have ridden up the chair lift at the Skiway on one of the chairs dedicated to Chuck Stone.

The 2014-2015 season is the last one covered in this publication. Over the years, due to excellent coaching, dedicated parents and volunteers, and hard working, talented ski racers, the Buck Hill Ski Racing Team has achieved

2011 Chuck Stone Winners, L to R: Maisie Ide, Paula Moltzan, and Sterling Grant

Nancy and Jessica Stone at the Chuck Stone Memorial Awards Ceremony.

unprecedented worldwide success.

There are some years when we just did not have information on the team members and the race results. There was a concentrated effort to make this brief history as thorough as possible. In 2015, at the time that this history ends, Jake Olson and Uros Pavlovcic were co-directors of the team and Erich was Executive Advisor and Hill Ambassador.

A special thanks to all the wonderful coaches who have contributed to making the Buck Hill Ski Racing team such a huge success. Because of all their hard work and dedication the team is still thriving today. We have already mentioned some of the coaches but wanted to make sure they were all recognized. Marion Polakiewicz has been the equipment manager of the team for the last 40 years. His steadfast dependability has been truly appreciated.

Calista Anderson	Walter Heustis	Robbie Massie	Kurt Reichert
Buzz Bainbridge	Jim Holst	Truck Morrison	Erich Sailer
Pascal Dalseth	Marty Huestis	Tasha Nelson	Martina Sailer
Andrzej Derezinski	Barry Jaeger	Todd Nelson	Ursula Sailer
David Fischer	Brad Kastner	George Neubauer	Maria Schilling
Erik Gabrielson	Alan Kildow	Doug Nordmeyer	Dominik Schweiger
Dave Gartner	Mike Larkin	Tony Olin	Polly Stone Hanson
Dave Grofscik	Erik Lempke	Jake Olson	Mark Thatcher
Greg Hall	Colby Lund	Uros Pavlovcic	
Kirsten Hayden-Cahoon	Connor Lund	John Peterson	
	Hilary Lund	Pepi Pittl	

Buck Hill moms volunteering in the timing booth at Mt. La Crosse. Top to Bottom: Judy Strand, Dawn Croasdale, and Andrea George.

Buck Hill mom Joan Larson volunteering during the Chuck Stone Memorial Race.

Kiltie Finsand, Maisie Ide, and Katie Larkin at the Marquette Championships.

Opening Ceremonies at the Chuck Stone Memorial Race. Carrying the flags are (front to back): Greg Larson, Doug Nordmeyer, and Tim Osgood.

Getting ready for a very cold day of ski racing at Lutsen Mountain. L to R: Taylor Johnson, Perrin Burke, Hannah Anderson, Madeline Wiltgen, Kiltie Finsand, Caroline Gagne, and Maisie Ide.

Kiltie Finsand and her mom Amy at the J3 Junior Olympics in Aspen, CO.

Buck Hill moms Judy Strand and Susan Whalen at the J3 Junior Olympics in Aspen, CO.

2009 Chuck Stone racers posing with lunch sponsor Chipotle's burrito. L to R: Paula Moltzan, Chloe and Laura Post.

Nicole Larson, Sarah Schleper, Madeline Wiltgen, and Erich Sailer at the J3 Junior Olympics in Aspen, CO.

Coach Uros Pavlovcic and Michael Ankeny.

Buck Hill racers Jessie Horness and Andrea Radke at Giant's Ridge.

Heidi Lindemeer getting some last minute tips from husband Steve at the Dual Dash for Cash.

Tip-top racer Todd Reget's winning style.

Kristina Koznick giving coaching tips to young racers at Kids and Koz Day at Buck Hill.

Alberto Tomba showing his stuff at the Tomba Lexus Tour presented by Rossignol.

A very early ski race at Buck HIll.

Young racers, including Polly Stone and Lori Greely, getting ready to go at Powder Ridge.

Local sportscaster Mark Rosen interviewing Jean-Claude Killy at the McDonald's cup in 1974.

*Shirley Schoenbaurer, a patroller
who is always smiling.*

Buck Hill Ski Patrol

Historical Overview of the Buck Hill Ski Patrol

1954-2015

Gary Nichols

Scott Ohland

The mission of the Buck Hill Ski Patrol (BHSP) is to provide guests and employees of the Buck Hill Ski area with emergency care and rescue, and to promote safe skiing and snowboarding within the guidelines of the National Ski Patrol System (NSPS also known as NSP).

The BHSP is under the supervision of the Buck Hill Ski Area management and abides by the policies and procedures established by management. Area management has total responsibility for all operations conducted within the ski area. Patrollers are expected to conduct themselves in a professional manner that is a positive reflection on the Buck Hill Ski Area, as well as the National Ski Patrol System.

Ron Henaman, ski patrol historian and author of this account.

Nationally, the Ski Patrol Association was founded in 1938 by Charles M. Dole (Minnie). He was also a member of the 10th Mountain Division during WWII. He had set up a model of a patrol for the 1938 National Championships on Mount Mansfield. His model focused on ski instruction, trail construction, physical conditioning, and first aid. The National Ski Association president, Roger Langley, was so impressed with it that he asked Minnie to organize a National Ski Patrol.

The BHSP was founded and organized in 1956 under the leadership of Jerry Fredrickson, a Northwest Airlines pilot and ski instructor. He then served as

Stuart Campbell congratulating Jerry Fredrickson on his accomplishments.

Patrol Director until 1969. During the first few years, the patrol grew from about 8 to 30 members. Rescue equipment included a specially designed toboggan, a snowmobile "for fast access to an accident area," a couple of stretchers, multiple blankets, 35 plywood "quick splints," a long backboard, several dozen cardboard splints and an array of bandages and cravats.

The BHSP "office and first aid/ care room" since about 1961 has been located at the base of the hill

between the original main chalet and the ticket office. For many years, the Buck

Hill Ski School shared some space with the BHSP. Subsequently, the Ski School moved into a much larger, more comfortable facility when new accommodations were constructed at the northeasterly end of the property adjacent to the restaurant/bar in 2001.

According to John (Ernie) Ernst*, he and Gaius (Gay) Harmon were avid skiers and joined the NSP in 1961. From 1951 through 1960, they owned and operated the Snail Lake Ski Area. They became charter members of the Twin City Metro Ski Patrol and added several others to that patrol. Twin City Metro Patrol assisted many Ski Area Ski Patrols in this region with supplemental patrollers, even as far away as Northern Michigan. They assisted the BHSP with scheduled coverage on Sunday nights through about 1985. At that time, John said, NSP Officials in the National office decided to phase out all "Metro Patrols" such as Twin City Metro. The BHSP and Buck Hill General Manager agreed that the Twin City Metro patrollers provided valuable assistance and could join the BHSP by transferring their membership to Buck Hill.

Over the years, the BHSP office and first aid/care room has undergone other minor modifications, maintenance and painting. Storage lockers for patrollers' skis and poles were constructed in the early 1970s. Next, two very sturdy wooden bunk style, carts/gurneys were designed and built to hold portable stretchers, with injured skiers on top and with a storage shelf underneath. In the

mid-1980s, custom heavy duty steel brackets with wheels were fabricated that were attached to the stretcher carts to make them easy to move around while providing care to the injured. Also, during this time-frame, old wooden benches were replaced by custom benches with professional quality custom padded cushions and back rests. These were courtesy of Fritz Rodde*, former Patrol Director 1977-1981, an experienced craftsman, and a well-known and respected upholstery teacher at Minneapolis Vocational High School for 30 years.

Dave Friedman and unknown patrollers.

From 1988-1992, Ron Henaman, BH Patrol Director, researched, reviewed, and instituted two significant procedural changes for the BHSP, approved by the NSP. One involved chair (aerial) lift emergency evacuation procedures and technique. The second introduced portable, hand-held 2-way radio communication.

From 1956 thru 1988, the emergency lift evacuation technique ("body belay") was basically unchanged. That technique was somewhat awkward for some patrollers. For example, after an evacuation rope with the sitting device attached were put in place and raised to lower the customer from the overhead chair lift, the belay rope was placed under one arm of the patroller, then wrapped around the patroller's backside and controlled by the manipulation of the other hand and arm. Friction and a hand grip controlled the speed of the descent. Friction caused by the rope traveling around and across the patroller's jacket and through his/her grip caused undesirable wear and tear on clothing and gloves.

The new/alternative chair lift evacuation technique (NSP approved) for BHSP utilizes common, commercially available mountain/sport climbing gear. It was determined that this technique would have a higher degree of safety for both the patroller and the customer and cause less wear and tear on the patroller's clothing and body. The climbing harness used was easily adjusted to fit various waist and leg sizes, highly secure, and was reasonably comfortable to wear during this maneuver. One or two locking carabineers attached the harness to a figure 8 rescue-descender or mechanical automatic locking safety device providing superior rope control for the patroller. Additional training and hands-on instruction were required and provided ensuring that all patrollers became proficient in the use of this technique and equipment.

The second change introduced the use of 2-way radios for direct communication between on duty patrollers, a base station, and Buck Hill management. From 1956 through 1988, summoning a patroller typically involved relaying a verbal message multiple times from person to person and finally reaching a patroller, or a land line phone call to a lift operator that would relay a message to a skier or another person that could relay a message to a patroller. In discussions, Ron determined that 2-way radio communication would contribute greatly to the accessibility, efficiency, and professionalism of the Patrol. However,

Ski Patrol and Joel Vanderwaal

Ski Patrol, L to R - Back: Kammie Meyerson, Ron Schlank, Tom Roberts, Joel Vanderwaal.
Front: Mark Ernst, David Hurley

radios were expensive and funds were not available to acquire a sufficient number of radios to satisfy any scheduled duty shifts. A fellow patroller, Honorable Harry S. Crump, Hennepin County District Court Judge, mentioned the possibility of BHSP (a non-profit) receiving a donation of used radios from the Hennepin County Sheriff's Dept. as they were being replaced.

The BHSP did receive eight of the older, large, hand held 2-way units. Initially, there was some resistance to this change. A few patrollers felt that carrying a bulky 2-way radio along with the "fanny pack" full of first aid supplies seemed awkward and not really necessary. However, as our patrollers learned the proper radio use and became familiar with the units, they were universally accepted. As time passed, 2-way radios became an integral piece of equipment that everyone wanted to carry while on duty. Over the following years, the old 2-way radios were retired and replaced with newer units that were more reliable and significantly smaller in size and weight. Today, nearly everyone also carries their own personal cell phone or smart phone for personal communication and personal use.

In 1998, Buck Hill management determined that a top of the hill, centrally located Ski Patrol "shack" (later appropriately called Eagles Nest) overlooking the area would be beneficial. Patrollers occupying the Eagles Nest and observing activities on the hill could, in many instances, promptly respond to incidents throughout most of the area. The new accommodations were constructed along with a new lift operator's facility for the Quad Chair at the top of the two front runs, Milk Run and Crossroads.

At various times over the years, Buck Hill promoted special events. One such promotion that benefited the U.S. Skiing Associations youth programs featured Alberto Tomba, the 3 time Italian Olympic Gold Medal winner. On February 6, 2000, a dozen Buck Hill Ski Patrollers experienced a unique moment to remember. They met Alberto Tomba and gathered around him for a group photo. In the color photo, Alberto Tomba is wearing a yellow jacket.

Ski Patrol and Alberto Tomba, 2000

L to R: Bruce Schiemo, Ryan Schiemo, holding award for Outstanding Student Patroller 2005-2006 season, and Karen Schiemo.

Dave Chlebeck, John Bukowski, Tad Conroy, Derek Renwick, Paul Anderson, Lisa Borneman, and Greg Snow.

Ryan Schiemo, Kasia Derezinski, Lisa Borneman, Tim Elness, Steve Jedlund, Kerstin Hammarberg.

Ken Wilson

Gary Nichols

Scott Thulien and Scott Ohland.

Western Region Outstanding Large Patrol 2005
Patrollers: (L-R): 1st Row: Peter Kay. 2nd Row: Jim Dwyer, Steve Pincus, John Bukowski, Kandra Thomford, Daryl Coons, Kerstin Hammarberg, Liz Luzum, MaryBeth Gullickson, Jeff Gullickson. Standing: Jim Rendahl, Paul Anderson, Lisa Borneman, Tony Anthonisen, Jake Meyer, Tim Elness, Scott Thulien, Bill Lappen, Sue Penque.

Patrollers, L to R: Jim Dwyer, Elmer Carlson, Jim Christianson, John Ernst, and Mike Beck.

Joe Downes

Jim Christianson, John Ernst, Bill Lappen, Friend, Mike Beck, Steve Pincus

Kerstin Hammarberg & Joe Anderson

Above: 2005 Buck Hill Ski Patrol; Below: 2015 Buck Hill Ski Patrol

Pete Dahl, Sara Dahl, Bruce Schiemo, Steve Sullivan, John Wareneke, Joe Downes

Ann Thulien, Joe Anderson, Julie Porter, Dan McEnery

Tim Aune, Brian Foley, Lisa Warshaw, Craig Banham, Jonathan Hoffmann.

Tom Poch

Patrollers, L to R: Steve Sullivan, John Warneke, Joe Downes, Bruce Scheimo, Pete Dahl, Sarah Dahl.

Modeling jackets from the past: Steve Pincos, Jim Dwyer, Mike Beck, Jim Christianson

Ron Henaman celebrating the ski patrol and the beautiful day.

From 1956 through 2015, Buck Hill has had 14 Ski Patrol Directors. In 1992, a plaque was created to recognize each director as they fulfilled their term. It was then presented to the membership during the annual patrol awards banquet. The plaque is mounted on a wall in the Ski Patrol office. The following list is current through 2015.

Jerry Fredrickson*	1956 – 1969
Bruce Lindgren	1969 – 1972
Tom Laitala	1972 – 1975
Mike Schmidt*	1975 – 1977
Fritz Rodde*	1977 – 1981
Don Swanson	1981 – 1985
Patricia Farnham	1985 – 1988
Ron Henaman (a)	1988 – 1992
Tony Anthonisen	1992 – 1993
Tom Roberts	1993 – 1996
Scott Young	1996 – 1998
Dave Krutzig*	1998 – 2004
Dan Bodimer	2002 – 2005
Kerstin Hammarberg (a)	2005

Note: The (a) indicates active, still patrolling with BHSP. The asterisk (*) indicates deceased. Dave Krutzig and Dan Bodimer shared responsibilities during some overlapping years.

Many additional plaques have been created to recognize individual BHSP members from year to year for their contributions or achievements during each ski season. These are hanging in the Ski Patrol office and aid room where they may be viewed.

Thank you Ron for this very comprehensive history of the Buck Hill Ski Patrol. Ron also had three nieces who were on the Buck Hill Racing Team. They were Jeanne, Nancy and Amy Henaman.

Memories from Friends of Buck Hill

I let it be known that I was writing a history of Buck Hill and if anyone wanted to add a memory of their own I would be delighted to put it in the book. After all, Buck Hill is all about the skiers and snowboarders and of course the employees as well. Here are the responses that I was so grateful to receive. Some other memories are incorporated in the main story.

It was a memorable occasion when patrollers Ginger Olson, Shirley Schoenbauer, and Pat Farnham came to ski with me in Red Lodge, Montana in 2008.

Walter Bush - Good legal advice from the start

Chuck Stone and I went to Breck School where we were teammates in both football and hockey. I graduated in 1947 and Chuck in 1949. We were also fraternity brothers at Dartmouth College in the early 50's. After several meetings in 1954, Grace Whittier decided to lease Buck Hill to Chuck. I became involved at this time and we formed a corporation with a board of directors of which I was a member. There were other legal matters as well regarding financing and insurance to name a few. One of the most significant happenings in those early years was the construction of Highway 35W right in front of the hill. I negotiated with the government attorneys regarding the "eminent domain" issue.

I continued to be a board member for many years. As Chuck went on to purchase Powder Ridge there were more legal matters of incorporation, government issues and so on. One of amazing things about Buck Hill is that a good number of Olympic skiers have had their start at a local, in town, facility that many of us have known as "Mont Le Buc." I remember talking with Jean Claude Killy when he was here for the MacDonalds Cup. On a personal note, I was an usher in Nancy and Chuck's wedding. I played a lot of golf with Chuck over the years. I would like to point out that the ski area began with one rope tow and one slope. Today it has 16 runs and offers not only skiing and snowboarding, but tubing trails as well and entertaining people from ages 3 to 85. Chuck would be proud.

Matt Clements - Current owner of Skijammers

Derek and I bought Skijammers in September of 2004. We both grew up at Buck Hill and on the Buck Hill Ski Team until 1986. Buck Hill has felt like home to us for 45 years. Skijammers does all of our pre-season instructor training in November and December and we bring kids there every Monday night in January and February as well as four Saturdays. Skijammers also visits Powder Ridge 4 times annually. I look forward to reading that history.

Nancy & Jim Countryman - Early owners of Skijammers

Jim and Nancy were former owners of Skijammers and very loyal and enthusiastic fans of Buck Hill. Nancy wrote this tribute to Chuck.

Chuck was the real reason why the Minneapolis/St. Paul area became a robust ski area for all of us living in the flatlands of the Midwest. Chuck saw a future in the Buck Hill area. Chuck gave of his time and money to make it happen. I called him the "Honest Abe" of the ski industry in the upper Midwest. Chuck might have been the CEO of Buck Hill but, never once did I ever feel that I couldn't call and discuss any and all matters with Chuck. He always was a great listener, always ready to help! Never was too busy to want to grow the sport of downhill skiing in Minneapolis... He never thought he was better than anyone else – he wanted everyone to have an opportunity to learn how to ski.

John (Ernie) Ernst - From Metro Patrol to Buck Hill Patrol

As metro patrollers we patrolled on schedule at about all the areas, even as far away as Northern Michigan. And yes, we scheduled into Buck Hill for Sunday nights. The national hierarchy didn't like metro patrols, so we got phased out in about '85. The few of us that were left, joined the Buck Hill patrol and skied Sunday nights. Two are still patrollers at Buck Hill.

I still ski with patrollers because they are my friends. They ski well, and they are good company. But I am not a patroller now and am qualified only to watch. But it keeps me involved with the patrol. So I want to say "thank you" to Buck Hill for being a very important part of my life.

Bruce Freeman - Crazy about skiing

My name is Bruce Freeman and I am crazy about skiing. My first time skiing at Buck Hill was in 1961 when I was 5 years old. I am sure I have skied there at least 500 times since and last year it was 14 times. My earliest memory of that time is a friend of my fathers, Roger Rozell, putting me between his skis and "bombing down" the Milk Run. I loved it and kept asking him to do it again.

I was a member of the Buck Hill Ski Team in the early 1970's and although I never became the greatest racer, I am forever indebted to Erich Sailer and his training which raised my abilities and confidence to a new level that I have enjoyed and cherished my whole life.

I have skied the Buck in every type of weather known to man or woman, from 40 below to hard freezing rain, 80 degrees sunshine (grass skiing in the late

70's), to an absolutely beautiful snow storm last year that found me in some knee deep powder (this is not an exaggeration) along the sides of Sailer's Chute and Sleepy Hollow. I had such a great time that night. I met all these fun people who were absolutely giddy about the powder. I replaced my father Harrison Freeman's long term on the board of directors in 2000. I consider it an honor and joy to help in any small way I can in this wonderful dream come true by Chuck and Nancy and friends.

Dave Freeman - First year member of the Buck Hill Team

I started skiing at six years old and at that time there was a J-Bar off to the left that served the easier terrain. I remember when my dad said I was finally ready for the T-Bar that went to the top of the Milk Run. I remember thinking how great this was and how nervous I was to ski down the "big hills." I remember almost living at Buck Hill as a kid and what a sense of freedom. I wanted to go and be with friends and ski for hours. In 1965, my dad got a call from Chuck that they were starting a ski team and he hoped my brother Frank and I would join. That first year there were 12 racers and we were coached by Walt Heustis and Dave Grofscik and this was a game changer for my love and passion for skiing which I still have.

My absolute favorite race that I remember like it was yesterday was at Lutsen, my junior or senior year. This was the last qualifying race before the regionals and I had fallen in the previous two races and needed a good run to make it to the next level. I was seeded 104th and the course had huge ruts by the time I went. It was a wild race as I jutted from rut to rut and finally fell through the finish line. Erich (now head coach) was standing at the finish line and gave me a big bear hug so I knew I had done well. It turned out I had the fastest run by almost a half second but I still had to make the second run. I was in seventh heaven. I was blown away by the roar of the crowd of people who had stayed late to watch my second run. I gave it all I had and ended up finishing third with my combined runs and qualifying to go on to the next level. What was really cool was all the parents that came up and congratulated me on this accomplishment of finishing third when starting back at 100+ starting seed and telling me that I had shown all the kids that had late seeds that it could be done.

My greatest ski racing accomplishment came in 1971 when I was the first racer from Buck Hill to qualify for the Junior Nationals. I made it in giant slalom which was picked first followed by Todd Reget, Mike Meleski and Cindy Stone who made it in slalom. Buck Hill put four skiers in the Junior Nationals at Mammoth Mountain that year and started the great reputation that Erich and Buck Hill have kept to this day as a racing power house. Since my racing days, I have been back to Buck Hill many times and I always find myself stopping and watching the racing hill and then finding Erich to say hello. I now live in Colorado and have seen many Buck Hill racers compete at events at Winter Park and it makes me very proud.

Frank Freeman – First year member of the Buck Hill Team

My brother Dave and I pretty much grew up at Buck Hill. We learned how to ski at Buck, ride a rope tow (two pairs of gloves per year and two rolls of electrical or duct tape), and the big reward of riding a T-Bar. We joined the ski team under Walt and then later under Erich. We worked off our season passes during our high school years by picking rocks, laying hay and painting just about anything. Our father, Ted Freeman, was in the insurance business and for many years wrote the insurance for Buck and became a territorial exclusive representative for a specialty ski resort insurance program.

Erich arrived my senior year of high school and final year on the team, he took me out individually to asses my skiing and racing abilities. In my memory he looked at me kind of sideways and yelled "vat is that you do with your arms, you ski like batman, no good, no good." To this day I am a bit conscious of my arms while skiing. In another year Erich would coach my brother Dave and others to the Junior Nationals.

I eventually followed in my father's footsteps and went into the insurance business. In 1986, I joined the specialty ski resort insurance program dad represented, Mountain Guard, and have been working with ski resorts on risk management and insurance services full time for the last 30 years based in Salt Lake City. In 1991, I became the program manager in the west and co-manager of North America. My early passion for skiing developed at Buck sustained me well through a career in the ski industry. I am very grateful for my early roots skiing the Ballroom and the Milk Run.

Margit Gerhart – A fashion statement and a lift-cident

It was one of the snowiest winters in Minnesota. The main lift was running, ready to carry eager skiers to the top of the hill - however, there were no skiers (we knew it was a bit nippy). I had come prepared with double-wafer quilted underwear - exclusively from the hunting department fashion section. My bibs were held up just by suspenders since it was impossible to zip them. I knew I could not afford to fall - getting up would have required a fork lift. The lift operator looked like a sleeping bag on legs, eyeing us not too enthusiastically.

Off we went, run after run, carving turns in perfectly groomed snow, humming a Viennese waltz. A fellow came out, skied 5 runs, went inside, and repeated this schedule two more times. Finally, he poled over and asked, "Do you ladies have any idea how cold it is?" We grinned and shook our heads. He looked at as, leaning forward on his poles and pronounced, stretching every syllable, "Minus twelve degrees!" Well, as I said before, it felt a tad nippy!

Undisturbed we skied some more, but after the lift operator let the chair hit our calves once too often, we decided it was time for hot chocolate. It would have been fun to hang out in the chalet but I could not take my jacket off without making a fashion statement (remember those unzipped bibs)?

Spring skiing at Buck Hill and for the occasion I had 'decked' myself out in a brand new outfit, white ski pants and a white/magenta jacket - wow!!! Everybody who could find an excuse was out at our favorite playground - Buck Hill. We had been loading the lift four across because nobody wanted to miss a run. I was lined up on the loading board with my husband and our friends, Tom and Uli Taylor. The lift came around, I lowered my bottom half, ready to sit down, when low and behold - a lady was sitting in my spot already! She must have lined up directly behind us, saw the lift come around, panicked and just plumped herself down. And there we went - I am sitting in her lap, my skis on top of hers - and the lift is taking off, the operator was too stunned to stop it at that moment.

I believe many of us still remember the little ditch right after the take-off ramp that in spring filled with mud. My husband tried to scoop me back up with the help of his ski poles, while grabbing my jacket. However, I tipped forward, pulling our friend Tom down with me, and landed in the middle of the ditch. Finally, the lift stopped. My husband and friend Uli, lowered themselves to assist us, with the lady still suspended in mid-air.

By then the lift line had increased. Right in front, several of our friends erupted in a chorus, waving their poles at our extra passenger, "Don't come back until you have learned how to ride a lift!" Our friend Tom, who was never at a loss for words, tried to lighten the moment by waving to everyone, while grinning broadly and announcing, "We will be back tomorrow!"

Since then there have been many "tomorrows" at Buck Hill. However, white ski pants have no longer been a fashion consideration

Bud Hirschfield - Enthusiastic investor

Bud wrote October 20, 2015: Back in the middle fifties, Chuck and Nancy Stone decided to open a ski area on a bump of a hill in Burnsville. I thought it was sort of nuts. Anyway they needed money and floated some one dollar stock for financing the project. Since they were friends of Nancy (my wife) and me, I bought 250 shares at a buck a share. I immediately wrote it off as a crazy idea and a total loss. Later they bought another ski area, Powder Ridge, then later sold it and I got some money from that sale. I don't remember how much. So I had to stop kidding them about "no dividend." Now they are selling Buck Hill and I am getting a big check for my shares. So what I thought was a total loser, turns out to be the largest percentage gain I have ever had on an investment I thought was a $250 throw-a-way. Thanks Stones!!

Roger Hoel - A father's story

Our son Gregory started skiing with me at Buck Hill when he was four years old. After years of teaching and skiing and spending many of the happiest moments of his life at Buck Hill, Greg died suddenly at the age of 42 from a heart attack linked with his 20-year struggle with diabetes. Buck Hill friends were kind and caring enough to hold a memorial service for Greg on a bright sunny morning in January of 2010 at the top of Crossroads Ski Hill. Ski instructors, patrollers and staff said a heartfelt and loving goodbye to a friend and fellow skier who felt as they do that skiing is like being in a Garden of Eden where the purity of skiing and the friendship of those who make it possible transcends the world we live in. As Greg's family got off the chairlift at the top of Buck Hill, Buck Hill Friends created an arch of ski poles for them to pass under as they approached a special evergreen tree for the memorial service. Many shared memories and sympathy and love. And there on that beautiful day in that beautiful place, we left some of Greg's dreams, prayers, heart, and ashes, knowing it was a place he loved with all his heart.

Dick Howell - A Southerner learns to ski

It was Chuck Stone who introduced me to skiing in the 1960's. The most snow I had ever seen before that was in Alabama when a Popsicle had been left in the refrigerator too long. The first real ski trip I took was with the Stones and we went to Deepwood Ski Area in Colfax, Wisconsin. Not only did I wreck the car, but I broke one of the Yugoslavian-model skis I had borrowed from the Buck Hill

Rental Department. But I persevered and later even came to own my own skis and boots. My oldest kids all became very accomplished skiers, thanks again to Chuck.

Heidi Hust – A chance romance

So glad you are taking the time to write a book about Buck Hill. My students always loved hearing about the history. Of course all of us old timers talk about the good old days.

David and I met on the chairlift at an early season instructor clinic in the winter of 1985. We married in 1991. Our kids were on the Buck Hill Ski Team. We started our kids skiing early so at 17 months they were out on the hill. Sure wish they had the magic carpet back then. Every year we took photos of the kids by the Mouse Pass sign so we could see how much they had grown. I have instructor friends who moved away but also had little ski racers so we got to see each other at races all over the U.S.

Dr. Buddy Ide – Racer and father of racers

I knew Dr. Buddy's parents and I don't know if they raced but they all loved to ski. In fact, we sat with Art and Nadine Ide at a Dartmouth Alumni dinner in early 1954 and Chuck talked about his idea of starting a ski area and they whole heartedly agreed. Their son Dr. Buddy raced and did very well. He wrote about his daughter Maisie who was on the Buck Hill Team at the same time as my granddaughter Madeline from about 2000 to 2010. Dr. Buddy wrote:

My daughter Maisie started racing at age 9 with Erich at Buck Hill. She was gung ho and I was very proud of my first skier. I anxiously asked Erich "what do you think?" to which he replied calmly "Well, she will first have to learn how to ski." My hopes were dashed quickly in the Austrian manner! Maisie cried on her first days at the area. First, she cried from the difficulty of riding the rope tow. I had to ride behind her and push her up the first few days. Then she cried even more from the fear of the daunting start ramp that loomed so high over the Burnsville skyline. Maisie later won the slalom at the Dartmouth Winter Carnival in 2015, along with many other college races for the Dartmouth Ski Team.

Gary Ladd – Rossignol Representative Extraordinaire

I grew up skiing at Twin Tows and Jake's Hill in New Hampshire, which were both cow pastures in the summer. After college, I worked patrol at both Sugar Bush, Vermont, and Mammoth Mountain, California. I first came to Rossignol in 1975 as a technical representative and moved to sales the next year. Rossignol's racing director had been speaking of Erich Sailer and the Buck Hill Racing Program since my first day there. It was worth the wait to experience the spirit of skiing that was in the hearts of all at Buck.

The race program which was becoming, and became, legendary, the ski school which never seems to stop working on skills, or the patrol which is always training. Buck Hill was and is a skier's hill! And over the seasons there was always a warm welcome from any member of the Stone family who might be at the hill that day or evening.

Representing Rossignol over the years and working with the Buck Hill Ski Team, watching athletes develop and move to the US or college teams, win National, NCAA, NCSA, World Cup titles, and later move to successful careers has been remarkable. I have wonderful lifelong friends that I first met at Buck Hill, all because of a love for the sport of skiing.

Many midwinter nights after the business day I would go to Buck to ski the late evening until closing. It was always special, and if there was no wind and a light snow falling, it became quite magical.

One special memory was the "Wonder Woman" performance of Jessica Stone spearheading, organizing, and ramrodding the Alberto Tomba event hosted by Buck Hill. This promotional event Alberto Tomba told me, and later told the Rossignol management team, was the best promotional event he experienced representing Rossignol on his entire North American tour.

Lastly, I met my wife Renee a ski instructor at a small ski area, Hidden Valley, just south of Green Bay, WI owned and operated by her family. Her father, Jack Frolick, started the area after returning from the Army in Europe where he was a member of the US Army ski team and raced in several races in which Erich Sailer was racing. They were at different ends of the starting order. Her dad spread a love of skiing to many generations of skiers in central Wisconsin. Our ski community truly is a "tight family."

Anna McCarthy - Getting an early start

In 2006, when Anna McCarthy was 3 years old, her grandfather, Charles McCarthy, thought it would be the perfect time for her to learn to ski. In Anna's own words (in 2015) this is how it happened:

I was three years old when my Grandpa, Charles McCarthy, brought me to ski at Buck Hill. At first I could hardly stand up but grandpa began teaching me to ski down the easier hills. When I was six years old I had a private lesson and by the time we were through I could ski every run. Throughout the years, grandpa brought me to ski at Buck Hill many times. He taught me how to ski with my skis parallel. We skied together and had a marvelous time. About half way through the day we went into the chalet. I had hot chocolate and French fries and my grandpa ate chili. Then we went back out for more fun. Now I race at Buck Hill every Monday night for two hours with the SkiJammers program.

Bill McCarthy - First volunteer ski patroller

Our heartiest congratulations to you, Nancy! You and Chuck really did a wonderful thing in building Buck Hill. I'm so happy and proud to have been able to be there at the beginning and watched the wonderful success you've enjoyed.

Doug Nordmeyer - Racer, pacesetter, and coach

Buck Hill changed my life. The opportunities, the skills learned, and the sheer fun, continue to pay dividends!

My first visit to Buck Hill was in the early 1960's. My friend's folks took us out to watch his older brother do some nice "Stein Eriksen" turns down Crossroads, feet glued together on his Head Standards. It looked pretty cool to me.

The following winter, we got our first season passes at Buck. Somehow we got involved with cleaning the chalet (vacuuming, table cloths, linen and garbage removal) in return for a free burgers and fries. That year, I had over 120 lift tickets for that $45 pass.

In 1969, I begged and convinced my folks to let me join the Buck Hill Ski Racing Club, with a new coach named Erich Sailer. In those days, Erich had us "hike" the hill for the first few practices, in spite of the fact that the lifts were running. He would also find the iciest snow mound and have us practice trying to edge on it. This was always comical, as skis did not have much for edges back then. Whenever Erich would set a new slalom course, with a "T" shaped steel bar, there would be a feeding frenzy at the start gate with everybody trying to get in the gate at the same time. It wasn't long before somebody figured out that with Erich on the bottom, you could just bypass the start all together, and get away with it. There was always chaos at the top, unless a coach was there...

In 1973, I was hired by Erich to be an assistant coach and by Chuck Stone to be the NASTAR pacesetter. NASTAR was growing fast and Mr. Stone let me keep all the re-run money and 10% of the gate. I won the Midwest pacesetting trials at Indianhead. Duncan Cullman was the national pacesetter.

Chris Omodt – Keeping an eagle eye out for trouble

My favorite memory from Buck Hill was in February 2009 when my daughter, Rachel Omodt, raced in the High School Sections meet and qualified for the State Meet, which was held the following week at Giants Ridge in Biwabik, MN.

I spent a lot of time at Buck Hill over the years. I started skiing when I was 14 years old and skied at Buck Hill for the first time in about 1974.

My oldest friend is Don McClure. Don and I met when I was four years old and we attended kindergarten together. Shortly after I started skiing Don started working at Buck Hill. I would ski with Don often utilizing his buddy pass.

I started working security at Buck Hill in 1998 after my kids started skiing. I continued to work security until the end of the 2018-2019 ski season. My daughter utilized my benefits over the years to train with the D-Team and then later to race for Burnsville High School. My daughter began racing varsity for Burnsville High School when she was in 8th grade. While she was racing for the high school I was a volunteer gatekeeper for all of the high school races at Buck Hill. I was also the chief gatekeeper for the first and second years of the Buck Hill Invitational.

Lastly, because of my love of skiing, I worked as a ski instructor for Buck Hill after I retired from law enforcement in 2012. Buck Hill has been a big part of my life!

No other word defines "skiing" better than the word passion, but it was the vision of Chuck & Nancy Stone and Glen Stanley that founded Buck Hill back in 1954.

Thankfully, passion and vision triumphed over sound business sense, because for those of us that have chosen to make our living tied to the ski industry, we learned long ago that the best way to make a small fortune in the ski business is to start with a large one...

In 1936, my grandfather Walter Pierce, founded Pierce Skate Shop & Trading Poster. In 1965, my parents John & Barbara added skis to the mix which led to the name change to Pierce Skate & Ski. I joined the business in 1980 and my wife, Terri, joined in 1985. Tyler Pierce (a former Buck Hill Ski Team member of 15 years) represents the 4th generation of the Pierce family to work at the shop.

In January 1994, Terri and I were guests of the Austrian Trade Commission at the 54th Running of the Hahnenkamm. It was at that point that I realized Buck Hill, with it's 309 feet of vertical drop and 45 skiable acres, was actually internationally known. Each evening a different ski vendor hosted a fantastic dinner with various current and former racers in attendance. One evening, the "Guest of Honor" was 1976 Olympic Gold Medalist and, at that point in time, the only 4-time winner of the race, Franz Klammer "The Kaiser." During dessert, he asked us if we were enjoying ourselves and if we had any questions. Since the opportunity presented itself, "The Kid in the Candy Store" started asking him one question after the next, until he finally looked at me and said, "Who are you and where are you from?" I introduced myself and indicated that I was from Minnesota, to which he immediately responded, "Do you know Buck Hill? Do you know Erich Sailer?" Absolutely true story.

Through the 90's, the legend of Buck Hill and the Buck Hill Slalom Factory continued to grow and it continues today. First, it was U.S. Ski Hall of Fame member Kristina Koznick and her 6 World Cup victories and 20 World Cup podium finishes, followed by Tasha Nelson, Sterling Grant, Michael Ankeny, Matt Strand, Paula Moltzan, and of course, the winningest female ski racer in history, Lindsey Vonn and her record setting 82 World Cup victories.

I am proud to say that all of the aforementioned racers were Pierce Skate & Ski customers and Buck Hill Ski Team members before they made the U.S. Ski Team.

The success of our shop is directly tied to ski racing; not only locally, but nationally. Without Buck Hill there would be no Buck Hill Ski Team and I would suggest there would be no Pierce Skate & Ski.

Eva & Marian Polakiewicz - Enthusiastic ski challenge and Nastar racers

In 1975, our Polish friend Andrzej Derezinski, who was assistant coach of Buck Hill Ski Racing Team, introduced us to the Buck Hill Ski Area and it has become our winter home. Andrzej was a member of Polish Alpine Olympic Team (Insbruck) 1964. Andrzej and Marian were NASTAR pacesetters at Buck Hill. Before he came to the USA Marian worked with the Polish National Alpine Ski Team as assistant coach for 7 years? He traveled World Cup races. For almost 40 years Marian has been working as equipment manager for the Buck Hill racing team. We have always appreciated Buck Hill's race friendly operation and we have participated in NASTAR and Ski Challenge races. In the old days you had to be in the top ten of your age group in the nation to qualify for NASTAR finals. Eva and Marian were invited four times and we were representing Buck Hill. In particular Eva remembers GS training with Chuck Stone. The course was set by Brad Kastner. I asked Chuck if I could ski the course? "Yes he answered – after you Eva." Chuck was really a gentleman. This was one of my best memories.

Scott Prochnow - Ski instructor and manufacturers representative

I attended a World Pro Ski Tour event at Buck Hill in February 1973. I was in college and a ski instructor at Powder Ridge with the ski school directed by Georg Nuebauer. Georg entered the race and several of us including his wife Maria, went along to watch. This was an amazing event with many of the great ski racers of the world competing – Jean Claude Killy, Spider Sabich, Moose Barrows to name a few. The Milk Run was set with side by side courses with three jumps for head to head racing. Photos of the event are on display today in the Buck Hill chalet.

I was involved with Erich and many great ski racers on the Buck Hill Ski Team, instructors in the ski school and employees in the rental department when I worked with Nordica. I brought a new Nordica race boot to Buck Hill for Erich and others to evaluate. Great reviews came in with Erich saying "best boot I have ever skied." It was a great feeling back at Nordica to have the approval of so many fine racers.

Mike Quinlivan – Early Powder Ridge racer

Mike wrote on the occasion of the Buck Hill Ski Racing Club being named USSA Ski Club of the year in 2008.

I just wanted to personally congratulate each of you and all the other past and present coaches, parents, club presidents, and Erich for 40+ years of leadership. My earliest memories are of Chuck Stone coming up to Powder Ridge on Saturdays and Sundays when I was 9 or 10 and actually getting to know the names of all us rug rats skiing out there and then sitting up in a booth over the loud speaker and counting down with a stop watch in hand the single pole race down the lower portion of Single Cedar. Erich, his coaches, Chuck, and all the other parents and kids were extremely welcoming to the Powder Ridge contingent at camps, training and races.

Shirley Schoenbauer – Devoted Buck Hill patroller

I first became a ski patroller in 1986 and envied the ones who came into the sport early and saw it evolve through the years. The ski patrol was started by Minnie Dole who had a friend that was severely injured but there was no rescue process at that time. Improvisation was the rule then, using wooden toboggans, splints of whatever was on hand. At the time of my joining, there was one room that was for booting up and treatment for what were called "victims" (we were not to call them patients) and anything else that was needed. A small hallway headed to the hill side which had a bench where two or three instructors sat that did not have a lesson. We got to know them well. Along side that was Bobbi Sipe's ski school office where customers signed up for a lesson. There was not space but we were expected to spend our time outside: patrolling! Even this space I understand was an improvement over the earlier years.

One man I would like to remember was Fritz Rodde. He was a patrol director for some years but this quiet humble man was one of those innovative, inventive contributors we don't even notices. He built cabinets at one end for our first aid supplies in the room and then there were the unique cots. I think he used army surplus folding stretchers covered with canvas that were fitted into a solid wooden base at waist height with foam cushion. The cot had a shelf below and the whole thing could move easily on wheels. He also made lockers that lined a wall for patrollers boots and skis. Various padded wooden benches appeared where needed. Most are still in use today. Even after retirement, if a rip in the cover happened, the bench would disappear for a few days and come back redone. One thing I noticed through the years was the kind of injuries. We often had "boot top" fractures and knee sprains/injuries. Also thumb sprains or fractures but with better equipment those injuries are seen less often.

We cannot forget the huge after school ski clubs. You heard "Oh no, it's Tuesday again – Olson Richfield Jr. High ski clubs are coming". Sometimes six school buses would roll in with hundreds of Junior High kids ready to rip. And they did. We did see a lot of them in the patrol room and sometimes in the woods and out of bounds areas. They received a package price through the school and I suspect some of the parents should have bought the lesson package. We got to know the chaperones quite well particularly, Tom Thomas, Dr. Marnie Law and a few dedicated other. Everyone always had a great time.

Bobbi Sipe – Ski school director from 1986 -1992

Our family started skiing at Buck Hill when our kids were very young. We had season passes and tried to ski at least once a week, always packing a lunch, trying to be practical. We got to know Sookie as well as Don, both were on the ski patrol. Don was a junior patroller at the time. Sookie ended up working in the office as well. Who could ever forget her custom made hats as well as her dedication to skiing.

Tom and I became instructors when Ursula was the ski school director and Erich the director of the Buck Hill race team. I will never forget the tryouts, the chair was not running and we had to literally boot pack Crossroads, do some maneuvers and then sidestep up to do another task. Erich was at the bottom with Ursula speaking German so none of us knew where we stood in the selection. Needless to say Tom and I made it and continued to teach at Buck Hill for many years. I call Buck Hill my stepping stone to my profession.

I also have fond memories of Gabe Cyr. We shared office space for a very long time and I hated the smoking so if I got to work ahead of her, I would hide her ashtray in places she could not find. I had a great amount of respect for her as she and her husband Oscar were a vital part of skiing. We laughed a lot and I still miss her.

Chris Stoddard - Executive Director/President of the Midwest Ski Area Association

Dear Buck Hill friends,

On the occasion of your 60th birthday, I wanted to wish you well and tell you how much Buck Hill has meant to me. When I was in school, my friend's uncle invited us to go skiing for a day at Buck Hill. Uncle Bob wanted to know how to ski and he went to one of the biggest slopes, abandoning Philip and me to the J-Bar slope. For me it was first chance. It was so much fun and Buck Hill was just the place and I came back again and again. As you all know, I have had a lifetime of working with ski areas and becoming a ski lift attendant at Sun Valley when I left grad school to try another path. It has been wonderful and I hope it continues a bit longer. I want you to know that Buck Hill changed my life and I am so grateful.

All the best,

Chris Stoddard
Midwest Ski Area Association

Emily Stone - Skier, snowboarder and granddaughter

Some of my favorite memories of Buck Hill are: Doing hair for the girls at the New Year Eve Party and having mine done when I was younger. When Dad dressed up as Bucky and went tubing with me. My first time going on a chairlift. My sister teaching me how to snowboard. The amazing donuts!! Getting snowboard lessons with my friend Heather. Doing my cousin Campbell's hair and seeing how much she liked it. Knowing that I am a part of an amazing family business started by my very own grandparents! And loving every minute that I was at Buck Hill.

Emily's older sister Jenny taught snowboarding at the hill.

Mike Stone - Enthusiastic Ski Challenge racer

Mike (no relation) wrote about how he happened to join a Ski Challenge Team. He had moved to Burnsville and was a skier.

Of course I noticed Buck Hill as I drove by on Highway 35W and I thought it looked like a great area for young boys and girls to learn to ski. However, it never occurred to me that I might enjoy skiing at Buck Hill as it looked too small, and then I met someone who challenged me to try giant slalom ski racing at Buck Hill. I had never done any racing, but decided to try GS racing at the tender age of 79. I was embarrassed with my awkwardness and my stellar time of 50 seconds to "race" down the GS course. Fortunately, I received excellent support from many skiers who witnessed my attempt to learn a new skiing skill. Gradually, my racing performance improved and I was invited by the Piste Off race team to fill a vacancy. I eventually earned a platinum medal. What a great day that was! Because of Buck Hill – I have many new friendships and great hopes of being able to ski and race there for many more years Thanks for the memories!

Paul Swanson - Memories of Chuck Stone at Buck Hill

My most vivid memory of Chuck Stone was one evening during racing practice. There was some "to-do" going on and some unhappy racers. My guess was that Eric, the racing coach, most likely had taken a snowmaking hose and watered down the race course to stiffen up the surface; the racers would have been happier on skates and not skis. Chuck had just arrived from work when this whole commotion made it to the ski shop/ski school area where I happened to meet him on the boardwalk. In spite of a long day at the office, and still sporting his tweed jacket with leather elbow patches, red necktie askew in the loosened collar of his white dress shirt, Chuck put on his boots and skis. He made his way over to the race practice slope, where, without hesitation, Chuck gracefully skied down the icy race course with precision around each and every gate, quickly dispelling any notions about the fairness or the impossibility of the conditions.

Jeannie Thoren - Women are not small men

Jeanne described her first Women's Ski Clinic held at Buck Hill, January 15, 1984.

I am from Marquette, Michigan. I'm a flatlander/ex-racer. I wrote a Women Skier Series for *Ski Magazine* in the early 80's. It explained my Thoren Theory, that women are NOT small men and need their own specialized ski equipment. I was ski bumming in Sun Valley, Idaho and was at the Duchin Room drinking beer and eating appetizers.....which also doubled as dinner at that time. I struck up a conversation with the gentleman standing next to me at the fireplace. It turned out he had actually read the articles with great interest. He asked if I would ever come to Minneapolis to do a Women's Ski Clinic? Absolutely!! It was Jim McWethy of the Ski Hut in Wayzata, Minnesota and Radar was the Rossi Rep who facilitated the demos. I had not been home skiing in ten years and had forgotten how shallow the slopes were. Jim picked me up at the airport and we drove straight to Buck Hill. I almost had a heart attack! I was used to testing equipment in the mountains! I though the women wouldn't be able to feet the differences I would be making to their equipment on such green/blue terrain. All l wanted to do was get back on the plane and get back to Idaho. As it turns out Jim did me one of the biggest favors of my life. Buck Hill proved to me that all you need is ten turns to know if you are in or out of balance. Location Location Location. I was terrified and it turned out to be the best thing ever. If you can ski in balance at Buck, you can ski anywhere the world takes you!!

Pete Wittig - Early local ski shop owner

Buck Hill has been a happy chapter in my life that still prompts fond memories. Every snow watcher who is exuberant about downhill skiing and now snowboarding will anxiously arrive at Buck Hill for the next run. In 1955, I took the risk of a lifetime, borrowing $500,000 from my grandmother and opened The Ski Shop on 43rd and Upton South. We ordered $250,000 worth of equipment for Thanksgiving opening and the invoices were due December 10. After four successful seasons, the Dayton Company purchased the shop and opened a ski shop in all their locations.

In 1962, I accepted my friend Dick Eincks offer to partner with me in a new ski shop venture. We made the agreement on a T-Bar ride to the summit of Buck Hill. In the fall of 1963 the Equinox Ski Shop opened at 500 Normandale Road. Business was good but about that time the big box stores made their appearance and definitely gave the smaller shops some intense competition. I gave up the shop in 1974 and moved my family to Sun Valley. Enjoy every winter. There are always some groomed runs at Buck Hill.

Marcia Young - A piercing party

Marcia was a college student who worked part time at the area at night and always had delightful stories about the teenagers that worked there.

It was a slow night at Buck Hill and the four midweek part time high school kitchen help decided this would be a perfect time to pierce each others ears. With ice cubes, darning needles, cork and alcohol in hand, they all traipsed to the downstairs bathroom. Half an hour later they all emerged with thread dangling from the opening in their ears. Mission Accomplished!

Afterword

We simply loved to ski. It was so different in those early days with our laced boots, cable bindings, ski's that were too long, and much lighter jackets. But I really don't ever remember being cold! Even so, I know we had as much fun as skiers and snowboarders do today. I hope you enjoyed this brief history of the Buck Hill story and I also hope you love the winter wonderland of Minne'snow'ta.